Springer
Berlin
Heidelberg
New York
Barcelona
Budapest
Hong Kong
London
Milan
Paris
Santa Clara
Singapore
Tokyo

Ulrich Immenga • Joachim Rudo

Unlimited Liability of State-owned Banks under the EC-Rules of State Aids

Springer

Prof. Dr. Dr. h.c. Ulrich Immenga
University of Göttingen
Department of International
and Foreign Business Law
School of Law
Platz der Göttinger Sieben 5
D-37073 Göttingen

Joachim Rudo
Johannesstraße 56
D-53225 Bonn

This publication is a translation of "Die Beurteilung von Gewährträgerhaftung und Anstaltslast der Sparkassen und Landesbanken nach dem EU-Beihilfsrecht", Nomos-Verlag, Baden-Baden, 1997.
We kindly thank Nomos-Verlag for granting permission to publish the English Version.
We kindly thank Wissenschaftsförderung der Sparkassenorganisation e.V., Bonn, for subsizing this volume.

ISBN-13: 978-3-642-95860-1 e-ISBN-13: 978-3-642-95858-8
DOI: 10.1007/978-3-642-95858-8

CIP data applied for

Die Deutsche Bibliothek – CIP-Einheitsaufnahme
Immenga, Ulrich:
Unlimited liability of state owned banks under the EC rules of state aids / Ulrich Immenga ; Joachim Rudo. - Berlin ; Heidelberg ; New York ; Barcelona ; Budapest ; Hong Kong ; London ; Milan ; Paris ; Santa Clara ; Singapore ; Tokyo : Springer, 1998
Einheitssacht.: Die Beurteilung von Gewährträgerhaftung und Anstaltslast der Sparkassen und Landesbanken nach dem EU-Beihilfsrecht <engl.>

SPIN: 10675271 42/3134–5 4 3 2 1 0 – Printed on acid-free paper

Foreword

The applicability of EC law of state aids to the state's unlimited liability for Savings Banks and *"Landesbanken"* is controversial. Legal and political discussions following the Maastricht-II-Treaty tend to assume that the liabilities have to be qualified as state aids.

This publication is based on the historical developments of German Savings Banks and *"Landesbanken"* as structural characteristics of public commercial activity. The liabilities in question derive from public ownership. Therefore, they have to be distinguished from securities provided by states for corporate debts which might be qualified as state aids under EC law. In this context the book discusses state aids to public companies and the private investor test of the EC Court of Justice. The authors question the EC Commission's concept to quantify refinancing advantages of *"Landesbanken"* which are supposed to be achieved by virtue of public liability. Therefore, the role of credit ratings in Germany, their influence on financial market decisions and potential legal consequences of ratings are examined.

This publication is a translation of a book edited in 1997 by the Nomos-Verlag, Baden-Baden, under the title "Die Beurteilung von Gewährträgerhaftung und Anstaltslast der Sparkassen und Landesbanken nach dem EU-Beihilferecht".

Ulrich Immenga/Joachim Rudo

Table of Contents

A. Statement of the issue

It can be gathered from statements of the European Commission and from relevant literature that guarantor liability and institutional burden, as instruments of creditor protection at public banks, specifically savings banks and *Landesbanken*, are to be understood as subsidies within the meaning of Article 92,1 of the EU Treaty[1] (hereinafter also referred to as the "EC Treaty"). Guarantor liability with respect to *Landesbanken* and savings banks is also being raised as an issue of subsidy law by the Monopolies Commission.[2] This is happening against a backdrop of increasing competition in the banking sector in view of the liberalization of national financial markets, the internationalization of banking, international deregulation through international agreements, the universalization of banking services, the increasing spread of comprehensive financing plans – also through insurance companies – as well as the trend for large industrial companies to go directly to the international financial markets.

The following study of the subsidy-like quality of guarantor liability and institutional burden requires a detailed description of the significance and function of savings banks and *Landesbanken*, and the related structural characteristics of institutional burden and guarantor liability. Within the framework of the subsidy test, this study will first examine whether the

---

1 *Cf.* "Konkurs unmöglich", Der Spiegel of 4-8-1996, p. 102; *Koenig,* EuZW 1995, p. 595; *Gleske,* pp. 313ff.; *Möschel,* Festschrift Raisch, p. 481, proceeds without further explanation on the assumption of a subsidy; taking the opposing view are *Schneider/Busch,* EuZW 1995, p. 602; *Scherer/Schödermeier,* ZBB 1996, p. 165, 172ff.

2 Monopolkommission, Hauptgutachten XI, 1994/1995, sections 113, 114.

assumption of liability connected with the continued existence of institutional burden and guarantor liability is, as such, to be understood as a subsidy pursuant to Article 92 I EC Treaty.

The refinancing advantages that possibly arise out of guarantor liability form the focal point of the discussion concerning the subsidy issue. In this connection, there is a discussion of the rating of *Landesbanken* and the question of the appropriateness of a rating for purposes of proving and quantifying a subsidy.

Finally, the presence of a subsidy is discussed in a case where an actual contribution of capital or a similar measure occurs for the benefit of a public financial institution in an actual crisis situation. The special characteristics of the banking sector with respect to possible governmental support measures for distressed banks must be taken into consideration in the subsidy discussion.

B. Institutional burden and guarantor liability as organizational concept of commercially active public institutions

I. Financial institutions under public law in the German banking system

1. The significance of public banks in Germany

The credit business in the Federal Republic of Germany is often described as a three-pillar structure comprised of private banks, cooperative banks and public banks. Further, "group competitive behavior" is assumed vis-a-vis private banks on the part of cooperative banks and savings banks, whose business activities are limited to their respective regions. The special tradition of public banks in the Federal Republic of Germany is evidenced by their significant share of the German banking market. In 1993, public banks had a market share of 51.8% in terms of volume, with 46.2% of the loans to domestic non-banks, and 52.7% of the loans to public budgets.[3]

In addition to *Landesbanken* and savings banks, federal and state special promotional banks and specialized financial institutions are also counted as public banks. These financial institutions with specialized functions exist both in public and private form.[4]

---

[3] *Cf. Dennig,* Wirtschaftsdienst 1995, pp. 210, 212, with reference to calculations of the Central Bank of Germany *(Deutsche Bundesbank).*

[4] In a report of the federal government on the investigation of shifting competition in the banking industry and on a safeguarding of deposits, Drucksache V/3500, 1968 (hereinafter referred to as "*Wettbewerbsenquête*" [the "Competition Study"]), p. 23, as many as eleven private and five public financial institutions were named.

Federal financial institutions were created primarily as special promotional banks for coping with the costs of the war. Counted among them are Kreditanstalt für Wiederaufbau (KfW), Bayerische Landesanstalt für Aufbaufinanzierung, Lastenausgleichsbank, Deutsche Siedlungs- und Landesrentenbank (DSL) and Landwirtschaftliche Rentenbank, which, as institutions under public law, are furnished with the institutional burden of the federal government, and to some extent also with guarantor liability.

The function of state special promotional banks is primarily to support housing construction and resident enterprises by means of loans with preferential terms.

The following reflections on subsidy law apply to savings banks and *Landesbanken*, but are predominantly applicable to other financial institutions under public law.

2. Functions and significance of savings banks

a) Historic development of savings banks

Germany's first savings bank was founded in 1778. The private "Ersparungscasse der Allgemeinen Versorgungsanstalt in Hamburg" had the function of accepting deposits from anyone and investing them as public debt in order to offer depositors a modest payment of interest. Thereafter numerous savings banks were established as private organizations by local communities as well. Today there are very few private savings banks in the form of financial associations, corporations or foundations. The most well-known example of the seven so-called "free" savings banks still in existence in private form is Hamburger Sparkasse.

In 1801, for the first time, a savings bank was established in Göttingen as a legally dependent part of the local administration.[5] Also as a consequence of the new corporate form, the number of savings banks in Germany grew significantly from 110 in 1825 to 3,133 shortly before World War I.[6]

Whereas initially savings banks were basically limited to deposit transactions and long-term lending, since the beginning of this century they have developed into comprehensive financial institutions. In 1908, savings banks were granted the capacity to be the drawee of checks, and hence permission to conduct current account and checking account business.

---

5 *Mura,* Sparkasse 1983, p. 69; *Mura,* Sparkasse 1995, pp. 88, 89.

6 *Cf. Pohl,* p. 229; *Mura,* Sparkasse 1995, pp. 88, 89.

The current organizational form for savings banks is based on an emergency decree from the year 1931.[7] The banking crisis of 1931 led to particular solvency problems on the part of savings banks, whose assets to a large extent were comprised of community loans. In order to reestablish depositor confidence, both the legal capacity of savings banks and the transfer of the separate property of the savings banks from the previously dependent institutions of the founding bodies to the newly founded institution of savings bank were ordered. Public liability continued to be in effect after the savings banks were made legally independent. Now the customer's contractual partner was no longer the regional authority, but rather the savings bank itself. A savings bank customer with a claim against the regional authority would have lost that claim when the savings banks were made independent, if not for the creation of guarantor liability as a substitute.[8]

The number of savings banks in Germany dropped from 879 in 1952 to 578 in 1990.[9] In the course of German reunification, numerous savings banks were newly founded, such that at the end of 1993, 703 savings banks with a total business volume of DM 1,331 billion were in existence.[10] In 1995, savings banks had a market share of the banking sector of 20.1% in terms of business volume, and 22.6% in terms of loans to domestic nonbanks.[11]

b) Functions of savings banks

The legal nature of savings banks as institutions capable of being the subjects of legal rights and duties under public law has been explicitly determined by savings bank laws in the German states.[12] The functions of savings banks are defined as follows in 3 SparkG (savings banks act) North Rhine-Westphalia, which is representative of other laws with similar language:

---

[7] Dritte Verordnung des Reichspräsidenten zur Sicherung von Wirtschaft und Finanzen und zur Bekämpfung politischer Ausschreitungen, dated 10-06-1931, RGBl. I, p. 537.

[8] *Cf.* Wettbewerbsentquête, BT-Drucks. V/3500, p. 48.

[9] *Cf.* Deutsche Bundesbank Monatsberichte, July 1952, p. 56; November 1990, p. 32.

[10] *Cf.* Handelsblatt of 4-7-1995 and 4-8-1995.

[11] *Cf.* Deutsche Bundesbank Monatsberichte, October 1995, p. 20.

[12] For example, § 1 SparkG Hessen, § 3 SparkG Lower Saxony, § 2 SparkG North Rhine-Westphalia, § 1 SparkG Saarland.

(1) Savings banks are business enterprises of local authorities or local authority associations charged with the function of serving the credit needs of the people and the economy, and particular of the business sector and of their guarantor.

(2) Savings banks strengthen competition in the credit business. They promote the people's sense for saving and their formation of wealth, as well as responsible behavior on the part of youth in financial matters. Savings banks contribute to the financing of debtor advisory services offered by consumer or debtor advisory bureaus; the guarantors determine the scope and distribution of these funds to the authorities of the advisory bureaus. The credit supply serves chiefly to provide credit to the middle class and weaker economic segments of the population.

(3) The business of savings banks, subject to their public mandate, is to be conducted in accordance with general business principles. The realization of profit is not the main purpose of business operations.

The original primary purpose of savings banks was to rouse and encourage people's sense for saving by providing everyone the opportunity for safe and interest-bearing investment of savings. As a result of the associated increase in savings rates in the overall economy, savings banks operate in the economic interest of the public.

By extending credit at favorable terms locally, particularly to the middle class and to weaker economic segments of the population, savings banks fulfill a supply function. Savings banks are supposed to prevent a situation where their guarantor's population – particularly in times of general strain and tightness of money – can turn only to profit-oriented banks, which are not prevented by law from changing and restricting the nature and scope of their business in the most different directions, even with respect to their own customers.[13] Savings banks ensure a continuous and blanketing provision of banking services, above all in areas that private banks will not serve due to profitability considerations. The extensive branch network consisting of more than 20,000 branch offices make it possible for all segments of the population to maintain current accounts, and hence to have access to cashless transfers.

Further, savings banks are required by law to accept all deposits of one DM or more. In some states savings banks are also required to open current accounts for everyone.

[13] *Cf. Schlierbach*, p. 54.

It is precisely this supply function that is being questioned in light of the very high bank density in Germany (by international comparison).[14] Since the rationale for state activity is to relieve shortages in supply caused by a failure of the market, the non-existence of any such shortages in supply is an argument for the absence of a public mission.[15] However, it is not solely a matter of actual market failure. Even potential market failure is sufficient, since savings banks can only meaningfully fulfill their function of providing comprehensive public services by means of long-term planning. This could not be achieved if savings banks were to retreat from an area of business every time an indicator for a market failure at a future point in time was rendered inapplicable because private banks relieved the supply shortfall with their own services.[16] In light of the high costs of entering the market, it is hardly conceivable that the state would fulfill its function of providing comprehensive public services by constantly entering and leaving the market, depending upon the current regional services offered by its competitors. Through their business activity, savings banks relieve any possible supply shortfalls that arise from potential market failure, and to this extent they fulfill public functions.

The character of savings banks as local institutions with local responsibilities is in keeping with the limitation of their field of activity to the region of their founding body, in accordance with the regional principal. With limited exceptions[17], they may only establish branch offices and conduct business within the territory of the guarantor.[18] Savings banks

---

[14] On this point, *cf. Möschel,* WM 1993, pp. 93, 96; *Hedrich,* pp. 94ff.; *Dennig,* Wirtschaftsdienst 1995, pp. 210, 212; according to *Kopper,* "Die Deutsche Bank ist in Europa nur eine kleine Regionalbank", FAZ dated 10-13-1992, there is one branch bank for every 1400 citizens in Germany, whereas in France, for example, there is one per 2100, in the U.K. one per 2700 and in Italy one per 3500.

[15] *Cf. Dennig,* Wirtschaftsdienst 1995, pp. 210, 212; *Möschel,* WM 1993, p. 93ff.

[16] *Cf. Gutsch,* p. 317, on the postal bank's function of providing comprehensive public services, which, with some qualifications, is comparable. *Cf.* also the book review of *Rudo,* ZHR 159 (1995), pp. 497, 499.

[17] *Cf. Schlierbach,* p. 94, on the establishment of branch offices outside of the territory of the founding body.

[18] *Cf. Stern/Nierhaus,* Das Regionalprinzip im öffentlich-rechtlichen Sparkassenwesen, 1991, on the topic of the regional principle.

must dedicate themselves to the welfare of their prescribed regional market, irrespective of its attractiveness for the deposit business or for the extension of credit. If the savings banks would cease to exist, business centers would receive preference, and a retreat from the region would be feared.[19] Thus savings banks and *Landesbanken* banks are viewed as a manifestation and a guarantor of a decentralized economic order, corresponding to the principle of federal governmental structure and of local autonomy.[20]

The significance of the supply function of savings banks is illustrated by the fact that they handle approximately one half of the current accounts in Germany, and cover over 60% of the financing needs of trade.[21]

In the ordinary course of their function as state-affiliated banks, savings bank are obligated to satisfy the credit needs of the public authorities, particularly of local authorities. Savings banks grant approximately 15% of their credits to public budgets.[22] However, they are not permitted to grant their guarantors preferential terms.[23]

The public mandate of savings banks is undergoing constant development. Particularly the corrective function in terms of competition policy is being ascribed ever increasing significance.[24] The function of savings banks to provide, through their presence in the banking market, increased competition for the benefit of consumers was expressly included in several savings bank statutes.[25] Savings banks in principle do not compete against one another, but rather compete as a group with private banks and cooperative bank associations. The function of this group competition in the banking business among the various institutional groups of private banks, industrial (*Volksbanken*) and agricultural credit cooperatives (*Raiffeisenbanken*), as well as savings banks and *Landesbanken*, was confirmed in the

---

[19] *Cf. Rehm,* WM 1993, pp. 133, 139.

[20] *Cf. Rehm,* WM 1993, pp. 133, 135.

[21] *Cf. Rehm,* WM 1993, pp. 133, 136.

[22] *Cf. Dennig,* Wirtschaftsdienst 1995, pp. 210, 212, with reference to calculations of the Deutsche Bundesbank.

[23] *Cf. Tiedeken,* Sparkasse 1984, pp. 286, 288; *Möschel,* WM 1993, pp. 93, 97.

[24] Reference to the increasing importance of the competition-correcting function is made in the government's 1992 proposal to amend the savings bank law of Baden-Württemberg; *Cf.* also *Klüpfel/Gaberdiel,* p. 89.

[25] *Cf. e.g.* § 3,2 p. 1 SparkG North Rhine-Westphalia; § 2,2 p. 1 SparkG Rhineland-Palatinate; § 6,2 SparkG Baden-Württemberg.

Competition Study (*Wettbewerbsenquéte*) of 1968 and by the Report of the Banking Structure Commission[26] of 1979.

The function of savings banks as provided for under state law has been explicitly confirmed under constitutional law. The Federal Constitutional Court (BVerfG), in its decision of September 23, 1994 concerning local autonomy and the function of providing comprehensive public services within the framework of Article 28,2 of the German Constitution (GG), affirmed again[27] that:

"Irrespective of the legal independence of savings banks, they have remained, due to organizational interlacement, local institutions with whose help communities and administrative districts can fulfill part of their function of providing comprehensive public services. In particular, they are supposed to rouse and promote the people's sense for saving, to provide them with opportunities to invest money securely, and to supply credit, with particular consideration for the middle class and weaker economic segments of the population."

3. Functions and significance of *Landesbanken*

Like savings banks, *Landesbanken-Girozentralen* are institutions under public law.[28] Their legal status is modeled on the savings bank statutes in almost every state. In each state the founding body of the *Landesbanken* is, albeit in varying proportions, the respective state, the respective savings bank and transfer bank associations[29], and regional associations of corporate

---

[26] Grundsatzfragen der Kreditwirtschaft – Bericht der Studienkommission, in: Schriftenreihe des Bundesministeriums der Finanzen, No. 28, Bonn 1979.

[27] BVerfG, decision dated 9-23-1994, WM 1994, 1971.

[28] Even though some laws in the German states speak of "public corporations", *Landesbanken* are to be regarded fundamentally as institutions under public law, *cf. Schlierbach,* p. 321.

[29] Saving banks and credit transfer bank associations exist in the individuals states as corporations under public law. In most states they are shareholders and guarantors of the *Landesbanken.* Savings bank and credit transfer bank associations also serve to represent the interests of local savings banks and to promote credit transfer transactions on the part of savings banks. The membership of savings banks is mandated by law. The savings bank and credit transfer bank associations are also the responsible authorities of a support fund for the institutional securing of savings banks (see Section B IV 3, *infra).*

bodies. For example, the Free State of Bavaria and the Bavarian Savings and Transfer Bank Association *(Bayerische Sparkassen- und Giroverband)* each hold a 50% interest in Bayerische Landesbank. Both are also guarantors of Bayerische Landesbank. Several guarantors of a single *Landesbank* are jointly and severally liable, independent of the size of their participating interest. For some *Landesbanken,* interests are held by other *Landesbanken.*[30]

The public mandate of *Landesbanken* is ultimately not definable, but rather is subject to constant change.[31]

Among the functions served by *Landesbanken* is their role as state-affiliated banks for state and local government banking transactions. That the focus of this business is the extension of credit to public budgets is demonstrated by the fact that within the banking sector *Landesbanken* have a market share in this area of 27.1%, which is considerably higher than their 17.1% share of business volume and 14.0% share of loans to domestic non-banks.[32] *Landesbanken* serve the credit needs of local authorities to the extent those needs exceed the financial capacity of local savings banks.[33]

Within the framework of their role as special promotional banks, *Landesbanken* also must support the economic objectives of the respective states in their regional and structural policies.[34] The necessity of the presence of bank decision-makers and the dangers of increasing external control of local banking markets are cited as a justification for this.[35] Significance is also attached to the information function for the state with respect to market developments.[36]

---

30 For example, WestLB is a guarantor of Landesbank Rheinland-Pfalz (Rhineland-Palatinate) and of Landesbank Schleswig-Holstein. *Cf. Dennig,* Wirtschaftsdienst 1995, pp. 210, 217.

31 *Thode,* ZfgK 1994, p. 172.; *Cf.* also Rehm, WM 1993, pp. 133, 134; a detailed treatment of the public mission of *Landesbanken* in *Gruson/Schneider,* CBLR 1995, pp. 337ff.

32 *Cf.* Dennig, Wirtschaftsdienst 1995, pp. 210, 212, for 1993 with reference to calculations of the Central Bank of Germany.

33 *Cf. Schlierbach,* p. 323.

34 *Cf. Schlierbach,* p. 323, *Thode,* ZfgK 1994, p. 172.

35 *Cf. Thode,* ZfgK 1994, pp. 172, 174.

36 *Cf. Thode,* ZfgK 1994, pp. 172, 174.

The *Landesbanken-Girozentralen* serve as the central clearing offices for cashless transfers, and they administer the liquid assets of the savings banks. The relationship between *Landesbank* and savings bank can be characterized as a vertical division of labor through cooperation and specialization. Whereas the savings banks serve private customer transactions and business with the middle-class economy, *Landesbanken* are active in big customer and international transactions. *Landesbanken*, too, fulfill a supply function.[37] The interlocking principle and the division of labor between savings banks and *Landesbank* are an essential prerequisite for the successful execution of responsibilities. This includes in particular access to international capital and securities markets along with access to stock exchanges, which for savings banks, due to their size, would not otherwise be feasible. Working independently, savings banks and *Landesbanken* would not be competitive in the market over the long term. In particular, the complementary and bundling function of the *Landesbanken* ensures a comprehensive and competitive array of financial services, even for customers of savings banks.

Landesbanken are permitted to establish branch offices in other German states and abroad, and they are subject to fewer restrictions on their business activities than are savings banks. As all-purpose banks, they have become much more like commercial banks.[38]

For this reason, the public mandate of *Landesbanken* has been questioned.[39] This must be viewed in the context of the discussion regarding the privatization of public banks, which mainly concentrates on *Landesbanken*. In this context, increasing significance is attached to public banks in ensuring competition in the banking industry through the role of *Landesbanken* as a counterbalance to large private banks within the framework of group competition. In the event of privatization, an increase in concentration is feared in that the *Landesbanken* could be acquired by the big banks.

---

37 *Cf. Schneider/Busch*, WM 1995, pp. 317, 318

38 *Dennig*, Wirtschaftsdienst 1995, pp. 210, 213, is of the opinion that limiting the business of *Landesbanken* to their "truly public function" would halve their business volume.

39 *Cf. Dennig*, Wirtschaftsdienst 1995, p. 210, with additional references.

Irrespective of the academic debate, the corrective function as it relates to competition has expressly been adopted in several savings bank laws[40] and hence also applies indirectly to the *Landesbanken,* since they must support the local institutions in their responsibilities.[41]

The 13 *Landesbanken-Girozentralen* reported a total business volume of DM 1,262 million in August 1995.[42]

4. The profit realization principle rather than the profit maximization principle

The pursuit of public functions is not precluded by the fact that public banks also adhere to the profit realization principle in their market activities.

It is of course true that according to German constitutional law business undertaken by the state for the sole purpose of realizing a profit cannot be a legitimate exercise of a public mandate.[43]

The prohibition against an exclusive orientation toward the maximization of profit does not, however, preclude the taking of profits. The limitations imposed with respect to the pursuit of business interests do not relieve public enterprises from the responsibility of efficient management of their budgets; thus profit realization by some public organizations, for example the Central Bank of Germany *(Deutsche Bundesbank),* cannot be prevented.

Accordingly, savings banks and *Landesbanken* are required by law to run their business operations from an economic standpoint, but without seeking primarily to achieve a profit.[44] The federal government found on this issue[45] that:

"... public banks are not created for the purpose of earning high profits and distributing a more or less substantial portion thereof; rather they are there in order to serve a distinct special promotional function; however it must also be said that giving up profit maximization does not mean giving up profit realization as such.

---

[40] *Cf.* Section B I 2. b), *supra.*

[41] *Cf.* e.g. § 26,4 SparkG Rhineland-Palatinate.

[42] Deutsche Bundesbank Monatsbericht, October 1995, p. 20.

[43] *Cf. e.g. Reiner Schmidt,* Öffentliches Wirtschaftsrecht, p. 507; *Püttner,* Die öffentlichen Unternehmen, p. 131; *Emmerich,* AG 1985, pp. 293, 295.

[44] Wettbewerbsenquête, BT-Drucks. V/3500, p. 18.

[45] Wettbewerbsenquête, BT-Drucks. V/3500, p. 52.

From the standpoint of the founding body, it is consistent with abandoning profit maximization that it forgoes distributions of earnings at the level typically expected for use of private capital."

A decision of the Higher Administrative Court (OVG) of Muenster reads as follows on this topic[46]:

"The decisive emphasis of the business activities of savings banks lies in subordinating the quest for profits to its public objective and business activity, i.e. in the prohibition against declaring profit realization and maximization to be the sole or primary goal of business policy decisions."

The savings bank and Landesbank statutes universally hold that profit maximization may not be the primary purpose of business activity.[47]

One must distinguish the issue of profit realization or maximization from the issue of profit utilization.

Pursuant to § 10,2 No. 4 of the Banking Supervisory Act (KWG), for savings banks, the reserves are to be regarded as liable funds. Hence savings banks must form their own funds from their reserves.[48] The annual surplus must be allocated to the contingency reserves for the time being in varying amounts depending on the respective applicable savings bank statutes. In addition, some states provide for the creation of free reserves. Distributions to the founding body are permissible only if the reserves have reached a certain percentage of deposits (minimum contingency reserve).[49] Pursuant to most savings bank statutes, the profit paid out to the savings bank's founding body must be used for the public benefit.[50]

46 OVG Muenster, DVBl. 1980, p. 81.

47 For example, Article 4,3 LandesbankG Bavaria, § 4 LandesbankG Berlin, § 3,3 SparkG North Rhine-Westphalia all comment that the realization of profit is not the primary purpose of the business enterprise. § 4 NordLBG goes even further: "The pursuit of profit must be subordinated, to the extent the public interest so requires."

48 *Cf. Schlierbach,* p. 277.

49 *Cf. Schlierbach,* p. 281.

50 *Cf. Schlierbach,* p. 286.

II. Institutional burden and guarantor liability as structural characteristics of public commercial activity

1. Institutional burden

a) Origin and scope of institutional burden

Institutional burden is understood to be the obligation of the founding body *"to ensure the economic basis of the institution, to maintain the ability of the institution to function over the entire course of its existence, and to offset any financial deficits (adverse balance) through the use of subsidies or other appropriate means"*[51]. Hence it concerns the principle of the financial responsibility of a corporate guarantor.

Since 1982, institutional burden has been standardized in various laws governing savings banks. For example, 3,2 SparkG Rhineland-Palatinate reads as follows:

"The guarantor ensures that the savings bank is able to carry out its functions (institutional burden)."

Institutional burden is not an obligation with respect to a third party, who for example would be entitled to use it as the basis for a performance claim. Rather, it is solely the obligation of the state, the fulfillment of which, if necessary, could be enforced by the supervisory authority of the founding body[52]. As an instrument of institutional safeguarding, it is effective only with respect to the internal relationship between founding body and institution. Creditors cannot derive any rights of their own from institutional burden.

---

[51] Wettbewerbsenquête, BT-Drucks. V/3500, p. 47.

[52] Wettbewerbsenquête, BT-Drucks. V/3500, p. 48.

[53] PreussOVG, Decision of June 4, 1897, PreussVBl. 19, 1897/98, p. 280ff.; in: *Weide/Bosse*, I., pp. 267, 270; detailed treatment in *Koenig*, WM 1995, 821, 824.

[54] § 8,6 sentence 1 SparkG Baden-Württemberg reads as follows: "The guarantor ensures that the savings bank can carry out its functions." Similar formulations are found in § 5,3 SparkG North Rhine-Westphalia; § 3,2 SparkG Mecklenburg-Vorpommern; § 3,2 SparkG Rhineland-Palatinate; § 3,2 SparkG Saxony; § 4,1 SparkG Saarland; § 4,1 SparkG Schleswig-Holstein; § 4,2 LandesBG Hamburg; § 4,2 LandesBG Saxony.

Institutional burden was expressly recognized for the first time in 1897 by the Prussian Higher Administrative Court (PreussOVG)[53]. In the meantime, a majority of savings bank laws have implemented a positive regulation of institutional burden[54].

Institutional burden, even in the absence of positive regulation, is considered to be an unwritten principle of administrative law[55]. Upon the establishment of an institution charged with carrying out public functions, the founding body also assumes responsibility for the legal entity that has been called into existence, because otherwise the founding body would have to undertake those functions itself[56].

Institutional burden concerns the obligation of the founding body to prevent the occurrence of an adverse balance through the timely provision of sufficient funds. By this means, the smooth business operation of the institution is ensured.

Current losses are covered by the institution's own funds. The founding body is only obligated to offset the savings bank's capital impairment when the contingency reserve has been exhausted[57]. In this respect, the founding body's obligations are subsidiary; they come to the fore only if the institution should not be in a position to ensure profitability and liquidity on the basis of its own funds[58].

---

[55] This is the absolutely prevailing opinion, *cf. Thode,* Sparkasse 194, pp. 134, 135, with numerous references; *Rümker,* Festschrift *Stiefel,* pp. 607, 609; *Kirchhoff* NVwZ 1994, 1041, 1043; *Schwark,* NJW 1974, pp. 1849, 1853.
The argument against qualifying institutional burden and guarantor liability as matters of common law or as general legal principles is that in so doing the principle of local autonomy as set forth in Article 28,2 GG would be violated. If one wished to base institutional burden on common law, then the capitalization of savings banks, which previously had been a voluntary, autonomous obligation, would suddenly become, by way of the vehicle of institutional burden, a compulsory obligation; fundamental and comprehensive treatment in *Oebbecke,* p. 43ff.; concurring treatment in *Hoppe,* DVBl. 1982, pp. 45, 49; *Püttner,* DVBl. 1981, p. 844; *Koenig,* WM 1995, pp. 821, 824. The Federal Supreme Court has expressly recognized institutional burden (BGH of February 16, 1984, BGHZ 90, 161, 169 = WM 1984, 691, 693). The Federal Administrative Court (BVerwGE 75, 318 (324) = NJW 1987, 3017) has expressly left open the question of an unwritten institutional burden.

[56] *Cf. Forsthoff,* 25 II. 3., p. 496; Wettbewerbsenquête, BT-Drucks. V/3500, p. 47.

[57] On this point, *cf. Schlierbach,* p. 282.

[58] *Rümker,* Festschrift Stiefel, p. 613.

The form in which the founding body meets its obligation lies entirely within its discretion. The elimination of an adverse balance, for example, may be undertaken through a contribution of new (own) funds, an acknowledgment of debt on the part of the founding body, guarantees to prevent the devaluation of assets, or the contribution of additional assets.[59]

Because of institutional burden, bankruptcy is almost impossible for banks under public law and has never happened to date, to the extent it is not already precluded under administrative law, as for example under Article § 25,2 of the Implementing Statute to the Judicature Act of Bavaria (BayAGGVG).

b) Limits of institutional burden

Institutional burden implies a fundamental supply obligation on the part of the founding body. This is not tantamount to either a right or a duty of the founding body to keep an unprofitable savings bank afloat through continuous subsidies.

Savings banks must be run in accordance with business principles. Doubts as to profitability in the context of a long-term prognosis, which then would mean that the fulfillment of legally mandated obligations is no longer guaranteed, are grounds in almost all savings bank statutes for savings bank mergers. Rationalization effects and reduced costs are supposed to be created by means of the (compulsory) merger of savings banks, thus restoring the financial strength of the savings banks. Just such a possibility is provided for, for example, in § 31,5 SparkG North Rhine-Westphalia:[60]

"If for reasons of the public welfare it is necessary to form a special purpose association of savings banks, particularly in order to preserve or establish the financial capacity of the involved savings banks in the interest of the improved supply of the population and the economy, the Ministry of Finance, in consultation with the Ministry of the Interior, may set an appropriate deadline for the local authorities and local authority associations concerned to conclude an agreement with respect to the formation of an administrative union of savings banks."

---

[59] *Cf. Schlierbach,* p. 129

[60] Similar language is found in § 17,2 SparkG Hessen, § 22,1 and 4 SparkG Rhineland-Palatinate, § 31,3 SparkG Schleswig-Holstein, § 24,4 SparkG Mecklenburg-Vorpommern, § 22,3 SparkG Thuringia.

In principle, savings banks may also be liquidated if the founding body considers the savings banks' function to be no longer required.[61] The basis for the forced liquidation of a savings bank may be that the savings bank can no longer guarantee the fulfillment of its functions as mandated by statutes or by-laws.[62]

Thus for a consistently ineffective and unprofitable savings bank that cannot meet its legally prescribed functions, there is a provision for merger or liquidation. However in practice, as a matter of savings bank policy, little significance need be attached to the liquidation of a savings bank as opposed to a merger.[63]

Financial capacity, within the meaning of the provisions of savings bank statutes, and profitability of a savings bank are inextricably connected. The fulfillment of the savings banks' public mandate is therefore only possible through behavior in line with competitive market conditions.

The standing subsidization of an unprofitable savings bank is not possible and legally inadmissible. Institutional burden at most can serve to offset unforeseen events and short-term bottlenecks.

The fact that in principle the support of a savings bank by the guarantor may only be temporary is substantiated, for example, by § 30,4 SparkG Baden-Württemberg. It provides that any surplus is to be used to repay the services of the guarantor to the extent the guarantor had previously offset an adverse balance.

Institutional burden is thus restricted to financing obligations in cases where the affected institution is able to fulfill its public functions. Institutional burden does not obligate the founding body to further finance financial institutions that in fact have no prospects for being profitable. Profitability and the fulfillment of public functions are inextricably connected. Should financial support nevertheless be provided permanently to unprofitable savings banks, then this is undertaken outside the scope of institutional burden. Guarantor liability, as a subsidiary obligation, is unaffected thereby.

---

[61] For example, § 35,1 SparkG North Rhine-Westphalia provides as follows: *"Savings banks may be liquidated by resolution of the founding body after a hearing of the administrative board. The liquidation requires the approval of the Ministry of Finance in consultation with the Ministry of the Interior."* *Cf.* also § 5 SparkG Baden-Württemberg, Art. 14 SparkG Bavaria, § 4 SparkG Bremen, § 28 SparkG Saarland, § 33 SparkG Schleswig-Holstein, § 28 SparkG Mecklenburg-Vorpommern, § 23 SparkG Thuringia.

[62] *Cf.* Art. 15 SparkG Bavaria; § 30,3 p. 1 in conjunction with § 32,2 SparkG Schleswig-Holstein.

[63] *Cf. Schlierbach,* p. 86.

2. Guarantor liability

a) Scope and origin of guarantor liability

Guarantor liability is defined as a *"direct liability, based on statute or by-laws, on the part of a regional authority or an association under public law with respect to the creditors of a legally independent financial institution for all of its obligations."*[64]

Guarantor liability is specifically regulated in all savings bank statutes.[65] Unlike institutional burden, it is not recognized as an unwritten principal of administrative law or of customary law.[66]

For example, the following language is found in SparkG Lower Saxony:

§ 5 [Liability of the Guarantor] "The guarantor is fully liable for the obligations of the savings bank. The savings bank's creditors may only have recourse to the guarantor to the extent that they are not paid off from the assets of the savings bank."

To this extent, guarantor liability represents an instrument for safeguarding deposits. The guarantor is liable, directly and to an unlimited amount, for all obligations of an institution under public law.[67] The legal ground of the obligation is not material.[68]

The subsidiary liability of the guarantor is derived from the savings bank statutes. Recourse to the guarantor or guarantors is possible only when the creditors cannot be paid off from the assets of the bank.[69] The creditors have

---

[64] Wettbewerbsenquête, BT-Drucks. V/3500, p. 48.

[65] Similar language can be found in § 8,4 SparkG Baden-Württemberg; § 3 SparkG Hessen; § 5 SparkG Lower Saxony; § 5 p. 1 SparkG North Rhine-Westphalia; § 3,1 SparkG Rhineland Palatinate; § 4,2 SparkG Saarland; § 3,1 SparkG Saxony; § 4,2 SparkG Schleswig-Holstein; Art. 4 SparkG Bavaria; § 5 LandesBG Berlin; Art. 3 LandesBG Bavaria; § 4,1 LandesBG Hamburg.

[66] *Cf. Koenig,* WM 1995, p. 821, 828; *Schneider/Busch,* EuZW 1995, pp. 602, 603, with additional references; different view in *Thode,* Sparkasse 1994, pp. 134-35, for whom guarantor liability is the outward projection of the reverse side of institutional burden, and thus is mandatory for institutions under public law.

[67] *Cf. Schlierbach,* p. 125.

[68] *Cf. Rümker,* Festschrift Stiefel, p. 618 with additional references.

[69] *Cf. Rümker,* Festschrift Stiefel, p. 619.

their own direct recourse to the guarantor or guarantors. Thus guarantor liability, in contrast to institutional burden, concerns an external relationship. To this extent guarantor liability represents a kind of deficiency guarantee or indemnity bond.[70] However, it is not an additional liability, but rather the guarantor's own liability by virtue of organization.[71]

Guarantor liability is accessory, i.e. the guarantor is entitled to the same defenses and objections as the institution; to this extent it is more similar to a surety than to an independent guarantee.

Obligations with respect to subsidiary institutions of the respective financial institutions under public law are not covered.[72] They may indeed be covered indirectly by guarantor liability if the financial institution under public law submitted a comfort letter for its subsidiary.

Guarantor liability for savings banks arose from the 1931 legislative decision to legally secede, as a matter of public organization law, from the authority responsible for local communities. Until 1931, banking transactions were conducted by the regional authority. Unlimited liability on the part of the regional authority was connected to it.

The legal autonomy decreed in 1931 was designed so as not to weaken the credit solvency of savings banks. From henceforth the regional authority was no longer the contractual partner of savings bank customers, but rather the newly independent savings bank itself. A savings bank customer with a claim against the regional authority would have lost the right to that claim after the savings banks were made independent if guarantor liability had not been created as a substitute.[73] Thus the personal liability of the local authorities was replaced by liability for a third-party debt. To this extent, guarantor liability is to be understood as an offshoot of personal liability.

Simple amendment of the statutes in the respective states could restore the management of savings bank transactions to the local authorities themselves, with the consequence of direct personal liability on the part of the local authorities. To this end, different legal forms are available to the local authorities.[74]

---

70 *Wolff/Bachof/Stober,* Verwaltungsrecht II, p. 345; Koenig, EuZW 1995, pp. 595, 597.

71 *Cf.* Section D II, *infra.*

72 *Cf. Rümker,* Festschrift *Stiefel,* p. 620.

73 *Cf.* Wettbewerbsenquête, BT-Drucks. V/3500, p. 48.

74 *Cf.* Section B III 2, *infra.*

b) The relationship between guarantor liability and institutional burden

Institutional burden and guarantor liability are inseparably linked. Whereas institutional burden is a supply obligation of the founding body with respect to a public bank and thus relates to the internal relationship, guarantor liability with respect to the creditors of a public bank is effected as an *external* relationship.

In practice, the significance of guarantor liability is secondary to that of institutional liability. This was a finding of the Competition Study, wherein it is stated that "recourse to the founding body on the basis of guarantor liability is only permissible if the founding body fails to fulfill its incumbent responsibilities vis-a-vis its institution, particularly the duty to offset financial deficits."[75]

Guarantor liability is merely an outwardly demonstrated reinforcement of institutional burden. In practice it is applied only when the guarantor has decided to liquidate the institution. There has been no such case to date. Since 1945 the state has not once been called upon directly in its role as guarantor, since in all qualified cases it had already taken action on the basis of institutional burden.[76]

Thus guarantor liability essentially means only a formal, much less a material, improvement in the position of the creditors, because thereby the bearer of the institutional burden has only expressed in a particular form that it would fulfill its already existing obligations arising from institutional burden in such a way that the creditors do not incur any losses.

Guarantor liability always presupposes institutional burden, whereas institutional burden may exist on its own without guarantor liability. This is demonstrated by the fact that for many public banks of the federal government, only one institutional burden exists. There is no guarantor liability on the part of the federal government for public financial institutions established or supervised by the federal government.[77] This is true, for example, for Kreditanstalt für Wiederaufbau, as well as for Lastenausgleichsbank.

---

[75] Wettbewerbsenquête, BT-Drucks. V/3500, p. 50.

[76] Wettbewerbsenquête, BT-Drucks. V/3500, p. 49; neither has such a case of the implementation of guarantor liability occurred since 1968.

[77] *Cf.* Wettbewerbsenquête, BT-Drucks. V/3500, p. 49.

c) The chain of liability for financial institutions under public law

For public banks that are not supported solely by the state, there is a chain of liability that goes beyond the guarantor liability of a single state organization or regional authority. For example, for Bayerische Landesbank, Landesbank Rheinland-Pfalz and Landesbank Saar there is guarantor liability both on the part of the state as well as the savings bank and credit transfer bank associations in each state.

The regional savings bank and credit transfer bank associations, in turn, are supported by the savings banks of the respective states, which are liable for the liquidity of their associations.[78] And the respective local authorities, in turn, serve as guarantors for the savings banks.

Among local authority, state and federal government there is in effect a system of revenue apportionment and horizontal financial equalization or supplementary allocations, as the case may be. In the most extreme cases, a budgetary crisis in one of the states may give rise to a supplementary allocation from the federal government to the state. But the states, too, are obligated to support the federal government in an extreme emergency. This has been clearly established by the Federal Constitutional Court (BVerfG) with respect to the financial status of the Saarland and Bremen. In a decision of May 28, 1992, it is stated:[79]

"If one member of the federal community of states – be it the federal government or one of the states – finds itself facing an extreme budgetary crisis, then the federal principle is concretized in the responsibility of all of the other members of the federal system to aid the affected member, with the objective of economic stabilization on the basis of conceptually coordinated measures."

Thus there is a chain of liability for savings banks and *Landesbanken* that ultimately is based on different forms of guarantor liability and financial adjustment and that is more extensive than the liability of a single local authority or state.

---

[78] *Schlierbach,* p. 308, is of the opinion that the association is solely liable to creditors for the association's obligations. The association may create contingency reserves; if they are not sufficient, then the association can require that the member savings banks provide funds in proportion to their share of common stock.

[79] BVerfG of 5-27-1992, NJW, 1992 p. 2279.

3. Guarantor liability and comparable state guarantees in other member countries

a) Austria

In Austria there is guarantor liability of local authorities not only for savings banks incorporated under public law. Even for savings bank corporations (AG) that descended from municipal savings banks, the guarantor liability of the local authorities remains.

The Austrian Savings Bank Act *(Sparkassengesetz),* a federal law, contains the following provisions:

§ 1 (1) Savings banks are legal persons under public law established by local authorities or savings bank associations.

...

(3) Savings bank corporations are financial institutions created through the contribution of the business operations or a portion of the banking operations of a savings bank into a corporation.

...

§ 2 (1) Local savings banks are savings banks established by local authorities within their own sphere of activity and for which they bear liability. The local authority (liable authority) is liable as a deficit guarantor for all obligations of the savings bank in the event of insolvency pursuant to 1356 ABGB; more than one liable local authority of a single savings bank are jointly and severally liable. In the event of the insolvency of a savings bank corporation, the local authority (liable authority) of the savings bank that entrusted its business operations or the banking portion of its business operations to the savings bank corporation is liable in the same fashion.

Pursuant to 1346 and 1355 of the Austrian Civil Code (ABGB), the federal government as guarantor is also liable for obligations of the Austrian postal savings bank *(Postsparkasse).*

The regulations governing guarantor liability for financial institutions under public law in Austria are comparable to those in Germany. One key difference is that in Austria there is no institutional burden in respect of savings banks.

For the provincial mortgage banks *(Landes-Hypothekenbanken),* which recently were transformed from legal persons under public law into corporations, each respective state is liable as deficit guarantor, pursuant to 1356 ABGB, for all present and future obligations.

Since 1995, state mortgage banks in Carinthia, Styria, Vorarlberg and Burgenland have been required as corporations to pay a fee for the guarantor liability of the state. This liability commission totals approximately one per mille of the assessment basis for which those liabilities of the bank that are not otherwise secured serve as a basis. As a rule, however, the major portion of deposits are already secured by other means; this is approximately 80% for Vorarlberger Hypothekenbank AG. The basis for assessment of the annual liability commission of 1% for the Landes-Hypothekenbank Steiermark is derived from the average of liabilities minus state contributions and plus 20% of the contingent liabilities. For example, the liability commission for *Landeshypothekenbank Vorarlberg* is the equivalent of about DM 5 million per year.[80]

b) Italy

Pursuant to Article 2362 of the Italian civil code, shareholders holding 100% shares in a company are fully liable for the company's obligations. This regulation is also applicable to the state, to the extent it is a 100% shareholder of a company. A claim of liability pursuant to Article 2362 can be asserted by creditors even before a business is liquidated.

The unlimited liability of the sole shareholder in Italy goes beyond the regulations set forth in German corporate law since it also applies to corporations.

This provision was the subject of a subsidy proceeding in the "EFIM" case.[81] As a consequence of this proceeding the future applicability of subsidy law was limited to cases where there is a market oriented investor.[82]

c) Other state liability obligations for financial institutions in the European Union

Liability obligations for banks on the part of the state that are comparable to guarantor liability and institutional burden can be found to varying degrees in most member countries of the European Union. A list was made

---

[80] *Cf.* Wirtschaftsblatt dated 4-10-1996.

[81] Communiqué of the Commission pursuant to Article § 93,2 EU Treaty to the remaining member countries and other interested parties concerning a subsidization plan of Italy for the benefit of EFIM, OJ. C 349/2, dated 12-29-1993.

[82] *Cf.* Section D IV 3 c, and Section F III, *infra.*

in 1995 by the ratings agency Standard & Poor's.[83] It names Denmark[84], Finland[85], France[86], Italy[87], Austria[88], Sweden[89] and Spain as countries with state guarantees.

III. Guarantor liability and institutional burden as a consequence of the administrative organizational discretion of the state

1. Permissibility of commercial activity of the state

There are no objections under EU or constitutional law against banking activities on the part of the state in competition with private enterprises.

Article 222 EC Treaty does not affect property laws in the member countries. Regulatory property arrangements, i.e. the nationalization and privatization of companies, continue to be affairs of the member countries.[90] Thus in principle member countries are free to establish public companies, although they must adhere to Articles 85-94 EVG in so doing.[91] Thus the EVG does not fundamentally oppose commercial activity on the part of the state in the form of indirect activity with unlimited liability.

---

[83] Standard & Poor's Ratings Handbook, April 1995.

[84] The Kingdom of Denmark is liable for Mortgage Bank of Denmark, and regional authorities are liable for Municipality Finance Ltd. and KommuneKredit.

[85] Municipality Finance Ltd.

[86] The Republic of France is liable for Caisse de Dépôts et Consignations, Caisse Française et Développement and Caisse Nationale des Télécommunications.

[87] The Republic of Italy is liable for Mediocredito Centrale.

[88] The Swedish provincial boards and municipalities are liable for Kommuninvest i Sverige AB.

[89] In the Kingdom of Spain, there is a state guarantee for Instituto de Credito Oficial.

[90] *Cf. Schweitzer* in Grabitz/Hilf Art. 222, marginal note 2.

[91] *Cf. Hochbaum* in v.d.Groeben/Thiesing/Ehlermann, Art. 222, marginal note 5.

The constitutional requirement for state banking activity is that the pursuit of the public interest must be the primary goal. The sole pursuit of profits would not be permissible.[92] The legislature has considerable discretionary freedom in defining the public interest and in choosing the instruments appropriate to that end. In particular, the social welfare state principle provides constitutional legitimacy to public banking activity.[93]

The right of local self-government provided for in Article 28,2 GG in principle grants local authorities the right to engage in commercial activity through public companies.[94] The local ordinances of the states make commercial activity of the local authorities contingent upon certain requirements. The founding, expansion or takeover of local enterprises must be justified or even necessitated[95] by a public purpose. There is broad discretion with respect to the public purpose.[96] The absence of such a public purpose can only be assumed if profit realization is the sole objective.[97] Moreover, the nature and scope of the enterprise must be in reasonable proportion to the financial capacity of the municipality and to anticipated need.[98] Sometimes there is also a so-called "subsidiary clause" stipulating that "the purpose cannot be accomplished just as well and just as economically", or better, in another way.[99]

The local ordinances do not grant local authorities the right to undertake banking transactions. Savings banks are the only exception to this.[100]

---

[92] *Cf.* Section B I 2 c), *supra.*

[93] *Cf.*, among others, *Stern/Burmeister*, p. 100.

[94] *Cf. Gerke*, Jura 1985, pp. 349, 351, with additional references.

[95] For example, § 88,1 Municipal Code (GO) of North Rhine-Westphalia reads: "... urgent public purpose *necessitates* that the local enterprise..."

[96] *Cf. Reiner Schmidt*, Öffentliches Wirtschaftsrecht, p. 506, with additional references.

[97] *Gerke,* Jura 1985, pp. 349, 352; Hidien, pp. 74ff; *Reiner Schmidt,* Öffentliches Wirtschaftsrecht, p. 507.

[98] *E.g.* § 108 GO Lower Saxony, § 107 GO North Rhine-Westphalia, § 102,1 GO Baden-Württemberg.

[99] Art. 89 GO Bavaria.

[100] *Cf.* § 102,4 GO Baden-Württemberg as a representative example of the statutory regulations.

But the limits of public commercial activity imposed under constitutional and local law can only be legally enforced by competitors within narrow limits.[101]

In conclusion, there is no fundamental objection on the basis of EU law, the federal constitution, state constitutions or local ordinances to banking activity on the part of the state in competition with private companies.

2. Administrative forms and legal forms of public commercial activity

Various organizational and legal forms are available to the federal government, the states and local authorities for the performance of public functions by public companies.

On the local level, it is possible to perform public functions through direct local administration, indirect local administration or local administration under public law, with several possible organizational forms for each.[102]

Direct local administration may be in the form of municipal enterprises, publicly owned enterprises or other institutions lacking legal capacity.

Municipal enterprises, the most common form, are legally dependent parts of the local authority's property and administration, *i.e.* the local authority is directly entitled and obligated with respect to all legal transactions. Their organization is determined by the regulations governing municipal enterprises in the states. Municipal enterprises enjoy a certain independence from the rest of the local administration. Municipal works and transportation services are the most common examples of municipal enterprises.

---

[101] The prevailing view is that they are not legally enforceable. According to this view, the prohibition in local regulations against economic activity on the part of public companies was not designed to protect private competitors, but rather solely to protect the local authorities from economic risks. For private competitors this is simply a legal reflex. On the other hand, it would appear that a subjectively public right on the part of third parties is indeed specifically laid down and emphasized in the subsidiary clause in, for example, Art. 89 GO Bavaria; detailed treatment in *Gerke*, Jura 1985, pp. 349, 355f.

[102] *Schmidt-Jortzig*, Kommunalrecht, marginal notes 658-660; *Nikolaus Müller*, p. 269.

Publicly owned enterprises are fully integrated within the administration and are reported only as special divisions within the administrative hierarchy. They do not have their own budgets.[103] Examples of the – less common[104] – form of a publicly owned enterprise would be the municipal motor pool or printing office.

Schools, municipal theaters or museums are examples of local institutions being run without legal capacity; however, they are not commercial enterprises of the public authorities.

Indirect local administration through independent legal entities may be in the form of corporations under public law, institutions with legal capacity, or public-law foundations.

In addition, there is local administration *under private* law by means of corporations, limited liability companies, private foundations or registered associations. Wholly-owned companies or holding companies of the state are also possible. Partnerships are also a possibility, but in practice they are extremely rare.[105] There is an additional alternative, namely that private organizations be subsidized for performance of public functions.

Examples of public financial institutions with private-law legal forms are, for example, *Hessische Landesentwicklungs- und Treuhandgesellschaft mbH, Niedersächsische Gesellschaft für öffentliche Finanzierungen mbH or Finanzierungsaktiengesellschaft Rheinland-Pfalz.*

[103] *Reiner Schmidt*, Öffentliches Wirtschaftsrecht, p. 511.

[104] *Cf. Püttner*, Die öffentlichen Unternehmen, p. 59; *Nikolaus Müller*, pp. 435ff.

[105] For example, pursuant to 89 GO North Rhine-Westphalia, § 104 GO Baden-Württemberg, a local authority may only invest in commercial enterprises whose legal forms are such that the local authority's liability is limited to a sum that is in line with its financial capacity; a similar limitation is set forth in 65,1 No. 2 Federal Budgetary Regulations (*Bundeshaushaltsordnung*). Because of the possibility of limiting liability, which fundamentally also applies to companies under civil law, the legal form is considered to be permissible, *Püttner*, JA 1980, pp. 218, 220; *Gerke*, Jura 1985, pp. 349, 354. Others reject the permissibility of the legal form of a partnership based on the meaning and intent of the regulation, *Nikolaus Müller*, pp. 472ff.; *Engel*, p. 34. For a detailed treatment of the advantages and disadvantages of these legal forms, see Nikolaus Müller, pp. 472ff.

The operation of local public companies is possible, and also quite common, in several different legal forms. In addition to the organizational forms under public law of the publicly owned company, municipal enterprise, and institution with and without legal capacity, the private-law forms of AG, GmbH, registered cooperative, registered association or private foundation are also available.[106]

3. Administrative organizational discretion in the selection of the legal form

In making decisions with respect to the means of performance of public functions and with respect to the appropriate legal form, the state has broad discretionary power.[107]

The constitutional limits of organizational power are bound by the assignment of competence, the principle of provision of legality, and the fundamental rights of others.[108] The organizational forms under public law named in the constitution are not exhaustive. This has been affirmed by the Federal Constitutional Court:

"The constitution allows the competent organs of the federal government some latitude with respect to the organizational form of administrative institutions under its jurisdiction; thus to this extent the federal government is entitled to broad organizational discretion." [109]

The state has the freedom to choose to perform its function of providing comprehensive public services either by itself, or to transfer that responsibility to a legal person under public law or to a legal person under private law. The direction that is chosen is entirely dependent upon how a modern administration, which by necessity intersects with the commercial realm, can best accomplish the sovereign duties entrusted to it.[110]

---

[106] Detailed treatment in *Nikolaus Müller*, p. 83.
[107] *Reiner Schmidt*, Öffentliches Wirtschaftsrecht, p. 509.
[108] Detailed treatment in *Nikolaus Müller*, pp. 217ff.
[109] Decisions of the Federal Constitutional Court (BVerfGE) 63, 1, 34.
[110] Separate opinion *Wand* in BVerfGE 38, 326, 344.

The broad organizational discretion also applies to the states, which have a constitutionally guaranteed right to autonomy in matters of organization. Organizational power under corporate law for public commercial activity on the state level is only minimally restricted by the state constitutions.[111]

Article 28,2 GG guarantees the organizational jurisdiction of municipal organizations as "the legal power of the local authorities to exercise their own freedom of action."[112] Organizational jurisdiction entitles the local authorities to delegate a portion of their responsibilities to independent legal entities, or to establish private-law entities. The delegation of municipal responsibilities to private-law entities is an historical development. Public-law forms of independence developed only later. It is recognized that the local authority, by virtue of its independent organizational authority, may exercise its own discretion with respect to the legal and organizational form in which it wishes to perform its public functions.[113] The guarantee of autonomous administration gives the municipal administration broad discretion in choosing between a public-law or private-law legal form.

4. Preliminary conclusion: Guarantor liability and institutional burden as consequence of administrative organizational discretion

The state has at its disposal broad organizational discretion with respect to the choice of legal form for the performance of public functions. The decision whether a savings bank should be operated lies within the discretion of the local authority. Limits are to be found only in the requirements of local law.[114] The decision regarding the legal form of savings banks has been made for the local authorities by state legislators. However, through amendment of savings bank law, a state could change the prescribed legal form or leave that decision to the local authorities.

---

[111] *Cf. Nikolaus Müller*, pp. 258ff.

[112] *Schmidt-Jortzig*, Kommunale Organisationseinheit, p. 65; *Nikolaus Müller*, p. 269.

[113] *Gerke*, Jura 1985, pp. 349, 354; *Scholz/Pitschas*, pp. 129ff.; *Nikolaus Müller*, p. 269.

[114] *Cf. Schlierbach*, p. 72, on the question of the general municipal law requirements for the founding of a savings bank.

The organizational discretion of the states in the choice of legal form is not restricted by EU law, the federal constitution or state constitutions in respect of the issues explored in this treatise.

IV. Deposit protection systems and bank supervision in Germany

1. Objectives of bank supervision

Special bank supervision is justified in Germany as well as in other countries by the economic importance and particular sensitivity of the banking sector. The federal government has characterized depositor protection as saver protection and the protection of the holders of wage, salary, annuity and retirement accounts as "an urgent function of social policy" and as "a stabilizing factor for the highly trust-sensitive credit economy."[115] Through preventive measures, bank supervision serves to forestall general bank crises. Even the failure of a single large bank would result in a chain reaction. A suspension of payment at one bank causes the withdrawal of deposits at other banks. This results in a suspension of payments at these banks as well, which in turn causes a further reduction in the money supply, which can exacerbate recessionary trends.[116]

Significant instruments of bank supervision are minimum capitalization requirements and the obligation to maintain a deposit guarantee system.

2. Minimum capitalization requirements

In 10, 10a KWG, minimum requirements are established for the own capital of financial institutions under both private and public law. For cooperative banks, the members' uncalled liability is recognized as liable funds, and pursuant to 10,2 No. 3 KWG an additional amount is assessed. Even the demonstrated free private assets of the personally liable partners may be considered as liable funds upon petition pursuant to 10,6 KWG.

---

[115] Wettbewerbsenquête, BT-Drucks. V/3500, p. IX.

[116] *Cf. Mösbauer*, p. 254; *Möschel*, Banken und Wettbewerb, p. 473; *Bieg*, pp. 30ff. The danger of runs on banks is emphasized by the Commission in XXIV. Wettbewerbsbericht 1994, text no. 378.

For savings banks, the reserves are considered to be capital pursuant to § 10,2 No. 4 KWG. No corresponding additional amount is recognized for institutional burden and guarantor liability. This has been expressly prohibited by Article 4 of the Own Funds Directive dated April 17, 1989[117] of the EU Council.

Several local authorities filed constitutional complaints regarding the non-consideration of institutional burden and guarantor liability as "liable funds" within the meaning of § 10,2 No. 4 KWG. They considered this to be an infringement of their right of local self-government pursuant to Article 28,2 GG, because it allegedly impeded the savings banks in the conduct of their business, and the guarantors in the performance of their responsibilities. The Federal Constitutional Court did not find that the non-consideration of guarantor liability and institutional burden as liable funds constituted a constitutional violation and did not grant leave for an appeal.[118]

3. Institution and deposit protection systems

The Deposit Guarantee Fund established by the Federal Association of German Banks *(Bundesverband deutscher Banken e.V.)* serves to protect creditors or depositors in the area of private banking. Its purpose is to provide assistance in the interest of investors in the event a bank experiences threatened or real financial difficulties, particularly if suspensions of payments are threatened, and to prevent the erosion of confidence in private financial institutions.[119] The Deposit Guarantee Fund covers the full amount of deposits of non-banks, however only up to a maximum of 30% of the capital resources of the affected bank. Averaging all banks, this corresponds to DM 70 million with which each individual deposit of an endangered financial institution is secured.

---

[117] Directive 94/19/EG of the European Parliament and the Council, OJ. L 135 dated 5-31-94, pp. 5-14.

[118] BVerfG of 9-23-1994 = WM 1994, 1971.

[119] § 2 of the statutes of the Deposit Guarantee Fund of the Federal Association of German Banks

As a matter of insurance supervision law, no legal claims for damages may be asserted against the Fund.[120]

In 1994 the European Council issued a Directive[121] prescribing the improvement and harmonization of deposit guarantee systems in member countries. It provides for a minimum guarantee of ECU 20,000 per depositor. The EU Directive, too, makes no provision for legal claims asserted against the guarantee system. Liabilities to financial institutions are not secured under either the German guarantee system or the EU Directive. The justification is that private banks cannot be expected to pay premiums for the protection of their competitors.

The deposit guarantee systems for credit cooperatives, savings banks, *Landesbanken*, and for other public financial institutions through the Association of Public Banks go beyond the direct protection of deposits in the private banking sector. As early as the 1930s, credit cooperatives established assistance and guarantee funds that made liquid resources available or offered sureties for troubled member institutions.

In addition to guarantor liability, the regional savings bank support funds serve as a guarantee of savings bank deposits. These funds are a legally dependent constituent part of the assets of the individual savings bank associations. The guarantee funds of the savings bank associations serve to protect member savings banks, and not indirectly, to protect depositor savings. A savings bank association can support a member savings bank when the possibility exists that without recourse to the guarantor the savings bank would not be in a position to meet the demands of its creditors or to avoid an adverse balance.[122] Further, there is a liability network among the regional support funds through the guarantee fund of the German Savings and Credit Transfer Bank Association *(Deutscher Sparkassen- und Giroverband).*

---

[120] § 6,10 of the statutes.

[121] OJ. L 135 dated 5-31-1994, pp. 55ff. The Directive has not yet been implemented in the Federal Republic of Germany.

[122] For more on the provisions of the Savings Bank Support Funds, *cf. Schlierbach*, p. 313. *Cf.* also No. 2 of the Model By-Laws for the Savings Bank Support Funds of the Regional Associations: "A case for support can be assumed if a savings bank by itself is not in a position to avoid incurring a lost suitable to endanger the existence of the savings bank or to impede materially its development . . . A general banking crisis cannot serve as a case for support."

Notwithstanding the existing guarantor liability, the security reserves of the *Landesbanken/Girozentrale* at the German Savings and Transfer Bank Association serve as supplementary protection for the deposits of non-bank customers of the *Landesbanken*. The volume of the security reserves amounts to 1% of total deposits of non-bank customers for all member institutions.[123] The security reserves may be used to assist individual *Landesbanken* to the extent that it is necessary for the protection of non-bank customer deposits. The existence of the savings bank support funds and the security reserves considerably lessens the likelihood of a concrete implementation of institutional burden and guarantor liability.

In addition, the liquidity syndicate bank serves indirectly to protect depositors. In order to prevent bank failures, it can grant short-term loans in crisis situations to member private-law and public law financial institutions.[124] It makes financial assistance available in cases where basically healthy banks have encountered short-term liquidity problems. By so doing they help to prevent runs on banks and bank failures. The guarantee of deposits is thereby supplemented by limited institutional protection, even if this does not really constitute a guarantee of the continued existence of member banks.

4. State support of banks in the event of crisis?

Although bank supervision is primarily involved with preventative measures so as to preserve the public's trust in the banking system, one can proceed on the assumption that in an emergency, the state, for the public good, will support large private banks. The failure of a major bank would give rise to concern about the possible failure of numerous other banks and hence of the banking system itself. Due to the sensitivity of the banking system, state support measures for the benefit of major, economically important banks are thus to be expected. In line with the principle of "too big to fail", the prevailing view is that there is a de facto guarantee on the part of the state for

[123] § 3 of the by-law's for the Security Reserves of the *Landesbanken/Girozentralen*.

[124] *Cf. Nicklisch*, pp. 119ff. A detailed treatment of deposit protection in Deutsche Bundesbank Monatsberichte, July 1992, pp. 30ff.

major banks and large regional banks.[125] The idea of there being a constitutional guarantee of existence – derived from the social welfare state principle[126] – for private banks that are recognized as serving the public interest and thus are subject to special limitations, may raise doubts as a matter of regulatory policy.[127] But that will not be explored here.

In any event, § 47 KWG empowers the federal government to undertake temporary emergency measures by means of legal ordinances if it is to be feared that banks will encounter financial difficulties that could be expected to endanger the national economy, particularly the orderly flow of general transfer transactions.

Questions as to the class of addressees (i.e. as of what size does a bank qualify for state support measures) and as to the potential extent of these state measures are ultimately speculative.[128] Certain is only that private rating agencies, in the calculation of their ratings[129], specifically consider state support for major banks in crisis situations, and that the Commission's subsidy supervision to a large extent tolerates such measures, as in the case of Crédit Lyonnais and Banesto.[130]

5. Summary

In summary, it can be concluded that the guarantee of deposits and institutional protection in the three banking sectors of public, cooperative and private banks have similar structures, ensuring depositors a high degree of

---

[125] *Cf. Schwark*, NJW 1974, pp. 1849, 1854; *Möschel*, Das Wirtschaftsrecht der Banken, p. 253.

[126] This view is expressed in *Schwark*, NJW 1974, pp. 1849, 1854.

[127] Detailed treatment of the doubts surrounding a guarantee of existence in *Bieg*, pp. 34ff.; *cf.* also *Mösbauer*, pp. 254ff., *Krümmel*, KuK 1975, pp. 524, 530.

[128] § 47 KWG, among other things, provides for the possibility of a moratorium for a credit institute in order to prevent a feared continued withdrawal of funds and to give the bank an opportunity to undertake necessary stabilization measures. *Cf. Reischauer/Kleinhans*, Kreditwesengesetz (KWG), Kommentar, § 47 text no. 5.

[129] See Section E III 3 d) aa), *infra*.

[130] Detailed treatment in Section G II 1, *infra*.

security.[131] The extensive – by international comparison – supply of the funds[132] as well as the existence of a liquidity syndicate bank and the de facto state support of major private banks make bank insolvencies in the German banking sector unlikely. This is acknowledged in the international financial markets.

[131] *Cf. Möschel*, WM 1993, pp. 93, 98.
[132] *Cf. Möschel*, WM 1993, pp. 93, 98.

C. Applicability of Article 92 EC Treaty

I. The concept of subsidies

According to Article 92,1 EC Treaty, "state subsidies or subsidies of any kind granted from state funds that distort or threaten to distort competition by showing preference for a specific company or industry are not compatible with the Common Market to the extent they restrict trade between member countries."

The term "subsidy" is not defined in EU law. Because of the phrase "subsidies of any kind", the concept of subsidies has been broadly interpreted by the courts, the Commission and legal scholarship.[133] Any attempt at a more precise definition would by necessity result in narrowing the concept of subsidies.[134] Thus even the court's definition, which characterizes a subsidy as a measure undertaken to achieve a specific goal that as a rule would not be achievable without outside assistance[135], cannot be conclusive.

Subsidies are characterized by the fact that they afford the beneficiary a gratuitous economic advantage.[136] Thus the concept of subsidies not only encompasses positive benefits, but also measures that mitigate a company's financial burdens.[137] The key determining factor for a subsidy is solely its beneficial effect; the (public) purpose being pursued

[133] *Wenig* in v.d.Groeben/Thiesing/Ehlermann, Art. 92, marginal note 4, with additional references.

[134] Thus *Lefèvre*, p. 112.

[135] European Court of Justice dated 2-23-1961, Rs. 30/59, Steenkolenmijnen, Judgement 1961, 1, 7; *cf. Wenig* in v.d.Groeben/Thiesing/Ehlermann, Art. 92, marginal note 4.

[136] European Court of Justice dated 3-22-1977, Rs. 78/76, Steinike and Weinlig, Judgement 1977, 595, 611.

[137] European Court of Justice dated 2-23-1961, Rs. 30/59, Steenkolenmijnen, Judgement 1961, 1, 42-43.

is irrelevant.[138] Neither is a particular form of subsidy required. The subsidy rules apply to both products and services.

The public institution from which subsidies are granted has no bearing on the nature of a subsidy per se. Article 92 applies even to subsidies by domestic, autonomous sovereigns, which as such are not contractual parties to the EC Treaty – for example the German states and local authorities. It is up to the member countries themselves to enforce EU law on the respective sovereigns.[139]

A subsidy does not necessarily presuppose an already accrued financial burden on the budget of member countries or other sovereigns. It is sufficient if the subsidy can lead to such a financial burden.

The requirement that support be given to a *specific* company or industry prevents general supports (i.e. general economic policy measures that benefit all companies) from being subject to a subsidy prohibition.[140] Hence general tax reductions do not constitute subsidies within the meaning of Article 92 EC Treaty.[141]

The presence of a subsidy assumes unilaterality, *i.e.* the absence of a consideration on the part of the beneficiary. In the event that a consideration does in fact exist but does not correspond to the value of the state action, some scholarship still finds that this precludes a subsidy. It is argued that subsidies must by definition be gratuitous.[142] But this would mean that contrary to the generally accepted practice of broad interpretation of the subsidy concept, wide areas of státe benefaction would not be covered by Art. 92.

---

[138] European Court of Justice dated 7-2-1974, Rs. 173/73, Italy/Commission, Judgement 1974, 709, 718; European Court of Justice dated 2-24-1987, Rs. 310/85, Deufil, Judgement 1987, 901, 923; *Müller-Graff* ZHR 152 (1988), p. 403, 416; *Wenig* in v.d. Groeben/Thiesing/Ehlermann Art. 92, marginal note 2; *v. Wallenberg* in Grabitz/Hilf Art. 92 EC Treaty, marginal note 6; *Rawlinson* in *Lenz* Art. 92, marginal note 2.

[139] *Cf.* European Court of Justice dated 10-14-1987, Rs. 248/84, Germany/Commission, Judgement 1987, 4013; *cf.* also *Wenig* in v.d. Groeben/Thiesing/Ehlermann Art. 92, marginal note 8.

[140] *Wenig* in v.d. Groeben/Thiesing/Ehlermann Art. 92, marginal note 16.

[141] *Rawlinson* in Lenz Art. 92, marginal note 8.

[142] *Götz*, Recht der Wirtschaftssubventionen, 1966, pp. 105f.; *Schina*, marginal note 50.

Hence for purposes of definition it is imperative that the payment not be compensated by the beneficiary with a corresponding consideration customary on the particular market. If the state measure corresponds to a normal commercial event or if a sufficient and customary consideration for the state action ensues on the part of the company, then there is no subsidy.[143]

The presence of a subsidy is not precluded by the fact that a measure is designed to offset disadvantages, for example disadvantages associated with a company's location.[144] The determination of a benefit is undertaken through comparison with the recipient's situation absent the subsidy. The situation of competitors is irrelevant.

Reference points for determining the presence of a subsidy can be derived from the goal associated with a given measure. At the very least, the goal may be viewed as an indicator.[145] This is particularly evident in connection with maintenance subsidies, where at issue is the continuation of a company that is no longer viable in order to preserve jobs.[146] If state support or measures are based solely on social or regional policy grounds and are not economically motivated, then one may assume the presence of a subsidy.

Article 92,1 should be construed as a general blocking statute.[147] It is mitigated by legal exceptions in Article 92,2 and by the possibility for Commission and Council to approve subsidies under 3.

II. Control measures of subsidy supervision

In subsidy law one must distinguish between existing and planned subsidies. Existing subsidies, which were already granted for a given member country prior to the effective date of the Treaty, or which were approved by the Commission thereafter[148], are continually examined by the Commission (Art. 93,1). They may only be prohibited effective in the future. For planned subsidies, the Commission must be notified immediately with respect to

[143] Advocate General Sir Gordon Slynn in European Court of Justice Germany/ Commission, Rs. 84/82, Judgement 1984, 1492, 1501.

[144] Decision of the Commission dated 7-29-1986, ABl. L 40/17, 18; *cf. Rengeling*, pp. 23, 30.

[145] Conclusions of the advocate general, *Lenz*, Rs. 40/85 European Court of Justice Judgement 1986, pp. 2322, 2330.

[146] On this issue *Ciresa*, pp. 62ff.

[147] On the prohibitive character of subsidies *Rawlinson* in *Lenz* Art. 92, marginal note 1; *v. Wallenberg* in Grabitz/Hilf Art. 92 EC Treaty, marginal note 1.

[148] *Rawlinson*, in *Lenz* Art. 92, marginal note 5.

their introduction or reorganization. Until the final decision of the Commission, the member country may not implement the planned measure. In the event the member country has already disbursed a subsidy that the Commission considers to be inconsistent with the Common Market, the Commission orders the member country to reclaim the subsidy.[149]

In practice, the emphasis of the Commission's subsidy supervision has been on monitoring crisis industries.[150] Subsidy control is designed primarily to prevent a "subsidy contest" in which healthy companies are forced out of the market by subsidized companies. Nevertheless, distortions of competition caused by subsidies that are not allocated to crisis industries or crisis companies are also subject to the Commission's subsidy supervision.

III. Applicability of Article 92 EC Treaty to public companies

Article 92,1 EC Treaty presupposes the support of certain companies or industries. Corporate form is irrelevant to the definition of the term "company" as used in Article 92, which essentially corresponds with the broad use of the term in Articles 85 and 86. It makes no difference whether a private or public company is at issue. This already follows from Article 90,1 and the associated Transparency Directive issued by the Commission.

In the Transparency Directive[151] a public company is defined as a company "over which the state authorities–through ownership, financial participation, by-laws or other provisions that govern the activity of the company–can exercise direct or indirect control."

Thus Article 92 is applicable to *Landesbanken*, savings banks and the aforementioned public financial institutions of the federal government.

---

[149] European Court of Justice dated 7-12-1973, Rs. 70/72, Kommission/ Deutschland, Judgement 1973, 812, 829; *cf. Rawlinson* in *Lenz* Art. 92, marginal note 10, with extensive references.

[150] *Cf.* Communiqué of the Commission on public companies, text no. 22.

[151] The most recent edition is Directive 93/84/EWG of the Commission dated September 30, 1993, amending Directive 80/723/EWG on the transparency of financial relationships between member countries and public companies, OJ. L 254/16 dated 10-12-1993. The legality of the Transparency Directive was affirmed by the European Court of Justice, European Court of Justice dated 7-6-1982, Rs. 188-190/80.

In applying subsidy law to public companies, consideration must be given to the special relationships between the state as the provider of capital and the companies as the recipients, and hence to the dual role of the state.

The court reasoned as follows on this issue[152]:

"Within the framework of pertinent statutes, private companies plan their production and distribution strategies with particular attention to profitability requirements. . . . Decisions of public companies, on the other hand – in the context of the pursuit of the public interest by public offices that can influence these decisions – can be exposed to quite different factors. The economic and financial consequences of such influence lead to a situation where unique financial relationships are created between these companies and the state that are different from those between the state and private companies."

To this extent it is also affirmed as a matter of subsidy law that in pursuing their public responsibilities state sovereigns make use of public or even private companies as instruments of state economic policy.

In addition to the consideration of state goals, the monitoring of subsidies for public companies raises particular difficulties because financial transfers to such companies can more easily escape notice.

Thus the Commission issued its Transparency Directive, in order to disclose the financial relationships between the public authorities and public companies through the imposition of disclosure requirements on member countries. The most recently amended Transparency Directive provides for a comprehensive and systematic reporting obligation for financial transfers to public companies. Among other things, the disclosure obligation applies to *"the sureties provided by the state to finance of loans (with details on the terms and all associated expenses paid by the company)."*[153]

If the state acts entrepreneurially, then as a matter of subsidy law there arises a dual role of the state both as investor and as enterprise receiving a capital investment. This is particularly problematic with respect to capital contributions and other financial transfers from the state to public companies.

---

[152] European Court of Justice dated 7-6-1982, France, Italy, United Kingdom/ Commission, Rs. 188-190/80, Judgement 1982, 2578.

[153] Art. 5a,2 of the Commission's Directive 93/84/EWG, dated September 30, 1993, amending Directive 80/723/EWG on the transparency of financial relationships between the member countries and public companies, OJ. L 254/16, dated 10-12-1993.

This includes both contributing capital as well as securing access to loans. It must be determined for these financial instruments whether they transpire under terms customary for the market, *i.e.* whether in its use of financial resources the state acted in a fashion comparable to a private company.

This private investor test developed by the Commission has been expressly recognized by the Court.[154] In one of the most recent decisions of the European Court of Justice regarding private investors, it is noted:

". . . that according to established precedents, contributions of capital of any kind to companies by the state may represent state subsidies if the requirements of Article 92 are met, and that in order to determine whether such measures have the character of state subsidies, one must examine whether a private investor of a similar size as the public administrative body would, under similar circumstances, have granted capital assistance of the same magnitude." [155]

This principle of the market oriented investor has been accepted in legal scholarship.[156] Similar principles can be found in other legal systems, for example in U.S. anti-subsidy law.[157]

The private investor principle has since been broadened in decisions of the Commission and the Court. The concept of the reasonable investor has been introduced that takes into consideration broader social and economic

---

[154] European Court of Justice dated 7-10-1986, Rs. 40/85, Belgium/Commission, Judgement 1986, 2321, 2345; European Court of Justice dated 3-21-1990, Rs. 142/87, Belgium/Commission, Judgement 1990, I-959, I-1012; European Court of Justice dated 3-21-1991, Rs. 303/88, Italy/Commission, Judgement 1991, I-1433, 1476.

[155] European Court of Justice dated 10-3-1991, Rs. 261/89, Italy/Commission, Judgement 1991, I-4437, 4459.

[156] *Wenig* in v.d.Groeben/Thiesing/Ehlermann Art. 92, marginal note 13; *v.Wallenberg* in Grabitz/Hilf Art. 92, marginal note 13; *Müller-Graff* ZHR 152 (1988), pp. 403, 420ff.; *Rawlinson* in *Lenz* Art. 92, marginal note 21; *Ciresa*, pp. 59ff.; *Nicolaysen*, pp. 130ff.

[157] U.S. Trade Agreements Act of 1979 (19. U.S.C. 1677(5)(B)(i)(Supp V 1981): "The following domestic subsidies, if provided or required by government action to a specific enterprise or industry, or group of enterprises or industries, *whether publicly or privately owned*, and whether paid or bestowed directly or indirectly on the manufacture, production, or export of any class or kind of merchandise: (i) The provision of capital, loans or loan guarantees on terms *inconsistent with commercial considerations*".

factors from a long-term perspective, yet without dropping profitability requirements.[158]

[158] *Cf.* D IV 1, *infra*, for detailed discussion.

D. Institutional burden and guarantor liability as a subsidy?

The liability of the state associated with institutional burden and guarantor liability might have to be evaluated as economic support of public-law banks within the meaning of subsidization regulations. This would require that comparable legal institutions such as sureties or guarantees that are not claimed could be construed as subsidies.

I. Sureties or guarantees as subsidies even in the absence of an actual case of liability

An unenforced surety or guarantee would not be a subsidy if one were to view a voluntary financial sacrifice from public funds as a requirement for a subsidy. This could suggest itself because neither unenforced sureties and guarantees in general, nor institutional burden and guarantor liability in particular, are associated with a direct burden on a public budget. An outflow of funds takes place – if at all – only later. In the 200-year history of financial institutions under public law, there has not been a single case of bankruptcy.[159] An outflow of capital caused by liability to a third party has thus never occurred. In numerous other subsidization cases, member countries have made the argument with respect to unenforced guarantees that they did not constitute subsidies because there was no corresponding budgetary burden.[160]

In the context of subsidy supervision, however, one cannot focus solely on the costs to the subsidy grantor at the expense of considering the effect on the recipient. For other purposes this kind of subsidy or subvention concept may very well be useful. This is the case, for example, when the is

[159] *Twiehaus*, pp. 47f.

[160] *Cf. Petersen*, p. 14.

sue is the burden on public budgets, such as is the case for the federal government's subsidy report, which is produced based on the *cost* principle. The subsidy prohibition of the EU Treaty is intended however to prevent restrictions and distortions of competition on the part of the receiver of the subsidy. Thus the effects on the receiver are decisive.

Further, it must also be emphasized that the granting of a surety may indeed be associated with a balance-sheet relevant *expense*, even if no actual payment from liquid resources has been made. A sufficiently probable liability obligation arising from sureties or guarantees in fact may result in a balance-sheet relevant expense due to the creation of a reserve fund for uncertain obligations (249 Commercial Code (HGB)).

A subsidy therefore does not necessarily presuppose an existing burden on the budget of a member country or other sovereign. It is sufficient that the subsidy could lead to such a burden.[161] Thus state guarantees, although they have not (yet) led to financial losses, can fall under the subsidy concept as used in Article 92,1 EC Treaty.

This is also the view of the Commission. It found already in 1979 that gratuitous sureties or guarantees are subsidies within the meaning of Article 92,1 EC Treaty even in the absence of an actual case of liability:[162]

"The granting of state guarantees – of any kind whatsoever – represents a subsidy as such, regardless of whether the concerned state actually must compensate at a later time for a 'case of damage'."

In a communiqué of the Commission to member countries it is stated:[163]

"Even a guarantee that is not enforced can put a company in a position where it can continue its business operations and force from the market a competitor that did not have access to a comparable security."

---

[161] *Wenig* in v.d. Groeben/Thiesing/Ehlermann Art. 92, marginal note 11, with additional references.

[162] Decision of the Commission dated 5-18-1979, OJ. L 138/79, p. 30, "Sonderregelung für die Finanzierung von Investitionen zur Steigerung der Produktionskapazitäten der Exportunternehmen".

[163] Communiqué of the Commission to member countries, applicability of Articles 92 and 93 EU Treaty and Article 5 Commission Directive 80/723/EWG on public companies in the manufacturing industry, OJ. C 307/3 dated 11-13-1993 (hereinafter the "communiqué of the Commission on public companies"), text no. 38.

Even state guarantees based on statutory law were treated as subsidies in the EFIM and *Hibeg/Krupp/Bremer* Vulkan decisions of the Commission.[164] Thus a subsidy need not be constituted only by direct financial payments and tax concessions, but also by sureties or the assumption of guarantees.

II. Guarantor liability and institutional burden as liability by virtue of organization

Sureties and assumptions of guarantees are characterized by the fact that they are supplemental to the liability of a legal entity (natural or legal person). The liability for obligations of the legal entity is not replaced. Rather, its obligations obtain an additional security beyond that of its own liability. This is true irrespective of the legal form under which the legal entity's liability is determined. As is the case to some extent for private partnerships under private law, the liability can be unlimited, or also limited to the assets of the legal entity, as long as that entity is an independent legal person.

There is a beneficial effect in the relationship between liability and additional security through surety or the assumption of guarantee. As has been demonstrated above, this effect can be characterized as a subsidy within the meaning of Article 92,1 EC Treaty. But this is not true with respect to the individual liability of the legal entity.

Guarantor liability and institutional burden are liability rules that lead to an unlimited obligation, but do not add to another existing liability. Legal entities in this case are the savings banks and *Landesbanken*, as independent institutions under public law. We are dealing here with corporate forms under public law that are established as legal persons.[165] The public institution, even in the form of a legally independent institution, is assigned to a sovereign.[166] The sovereigns of the public financial institutions that are the

[164] Communiqué of the Commission pursuant to Article 93,2 EU Treaty to the remaining member countries and other interested parties concerning a subsidization plan of Italy for the benefit of EFIM, OJ. C 349/2 dated 12-29-1993; European Court of Justice dated 9-20-1990, Commission/Germany, Judgement 1990, I-3437, 3454; Commission dated 4-6-1993, OJ. L 185 dated 7-28-1993, p. 43, *Hibeg/Krupp/Bremer Vulkan; cf. Koenig* EuZW 1995, p. 595, 599.

[165] *Cf.* Sections B I and II, *supra.*

[166] *Cf. Reiner Schmidt*, Öffentliches Wirtschaftsrecht, p. 512.

focus of this study are primarily the local authorities and states in their capacities as guarantors. In terms of the law of private forms of association, they would be analogous to shareholders in a corporation.

It has already been demonstrated above that the public authorities are free to choose the legal form in which they carry out commercial functions. To this end the municipal enterprise or the public institution is a particular option. The organizational form of savings banks has changed. As has already been shown, until 1931 savings banks were operated as non-independent enterprises, with legal capacity, of a corporation under public law. From a liability perspective, this means that the local authorities as sovereigns were directly liable for the obligations of the savings banks. This liability was retained following the legal separation from the administrative authority and with the transformation into a legally independent public institution. Direct liability was merely modified such that institutional burden was supposed to largely preclude liability problems, and guarantor liability was accordingly placed in a subsidiary role. In this way, the sovereign entity responsible for commercial activity made allowance for the change in organizational form. Guarantor liability and institutional burden are thus forms of direct liability on the part of public authorities. In a report of the federal government on the investigation of shifting competition in the banking industry and on the guarantee of deposits (Competition Study of 1968) it is argued that an elimination of institutional burden would not be possible as long as the basic right of existence of financial institutions under public law was recognized. The public liability of the founding body is inherently linked with the public-law status of banks.[167]

Corporate legal forms under private law are analogous to the public-law form and liability. The sovereign corresponds to the shareholders. A partnership limited by shares is a legal form that combines the independence of a company as a legal person with the personal liability of the shareholders. The public authorities would also have the option to chose this legal form.[168] It exemplifies the possibility of unlimited liability based on guarantor liability and institutional burden as a principle of liability with respect to a single legal person.

---

[167] Wettbewerbsenquête, BT-Drucks. V/3500, p. 50, sentence V.

[168] *Cf.* § 303,2 Transformation Act (UmwG); see also Section D VI, *infra*.

The liability provisions for public savings banks and *Landesbanken* thus are not comparable to a surety or the assumption of a guarantee, which precludes their being categorized as subsidies within the meaning of Article 92,1 EC Treaty. Furthermore, the liability provisions as such also cannot be considered to be a subsidy. If the legal entity is directly liable in a case of commercial activity on the part of the state via a municipal enterprise, this does not constitute a beneficial act within the meaning of Article 92,1 EC Treaty. It is a case of individual liability. This quality is not lost when the commercial activity is separated out and transferred to a legal person for which unlimited liability is assumed. Individual liability is merely replaced by liability for obligations of the legal person.

The argument developed here for the inapplicability of the subsidy regulations to the direct or indirect unlimited liability for commercial activity on the part of the state does not mean that these legal forms of public commercial activity are immune to subsidy law. The definition of an enterprise as found in Article 92,1 EC Treaty would also be met by municipal enterprises. A subsidy within the meaning of this regulation can be considered to be present if beneficial measures are undertaken that go beyond the general liability. This is especially possible in the event of crisis. Under such conditions it must be investigated, using the (yet to be discussed) private investor test for both municipal enterprises as well as legally independent public-law institutions, whether there is indeed an instance of a beneficial measure that goes beyond liability (see Section F, *infra*).

III. Subsidy law and property right

Pursuant to Article 222 EC Treaty, the Treaty does not affect property right in member countries. This emphatic neutrality of the Treaty in the area of property right means in particular that member countries continue to have the option of transferring private property to public ownership and vice versa. Thus it is left to national regulations whether commercial activity is to be undertaken by private entities or by the state. A discussion of any existing limits lies beyond the scope of this study. It is evident, however, that although Article 222 EC Treaty specifically considers public commercial activity to be permissible, it does not exempt such activity from adherence to the rules of competition, and thus from subsidy provisions.[169]

[169] *Hochbaum,* in v.d. Groeben/Thiesing/Ehlermann, Art. 222, marginal note 7

Nevertheless, the question must be asked whether a substantial intervention into public commercial activity on the basis of subsidy provisions can be excluded on the basis of Article 222 EC Treaty.

Guarantor liability and institutional burden are simply the consequence of the separation of banking transactions from the direct legal authority of the regional administrative bodies. The application of subsidy provisions to liability for commercial activity in the form of a municipal enterprise or of a legally independent public institution would have to result in a limitation of liability. However, this path is not open to legally independent public institutions. In theory, guarantor liability could be suspended for new obligations. But institutional burden, which is effective only within the internal relationship, is inherent even to a legally independent public institution. Sovereigns have the legal obligation to provide adequate financing to ensure the fulfillment of public functions.[170] In order to restrict the liability of the state, commercial activity would have to be carried out in a private legal form with limitation of liability (AG or GmbH). However, even this approach would not preclude the possibility that liability could be imposed on the state as shareholder under corporate law.[171]

The state's ownership would not be affected by formal privatization. The concept of property right within the meaning of Article 222 EC Treaty goes beyond that of property rights in a narrower sense. It also encompasses the limitation of property use. The European Court has made clear that the related question of a violation of fundamental rights caused by an act of an organ of the EU cannot be adjudicated in any other way except within the framework of EU law.[172] In the same decision specific attention was given to the question of whether there was an impermissible limitation of property rights. In the case at issue, which concerned the prohibition against expanded cultivation, the question was answered in the negative.[173]

---

[170] *Cf. Wolff/Bachof/Stober,* Verwaltungsrecht II, pp. 302, 345.

[171] See Section D V, *infra.*

[172] European Court of Justice dated 12-13-1979, Lieselotte Hauer/Land Rheinland-Pfalz, Rs. 44/79, Judgement 1979, 3727, 3744, marginal note 14.

[173] *Loc. cit.,* marginal note 19. *Cf.* also the comments of the advocate general, Capotori, *loc. cit.,* pp. 3759f.

Banking activity of savings banks or *Landesbanken* would not be hindered by being carried out in a private limited-liability legal form. But something different can apply with respect to the public functions, which are pursued simultaneously and are inseparable. The fulfillment of the latter is only possible if profit maximization is sacrificed. Thus according to current legal precedents, it is expressly valid for the financial institutions under public law treated here that their activity be carried out with a view toward profit realization, but not profit maximization. Allowance for this orientation of the corporate interest can be made in a limited way, at best, in the form of a corporation. The conventional public-law legal form is justified precisely by the necessity of pursuing profit-making interests to only a limited extent, in light of public functions.[174] On the other hand, one must keep in mind that corporation law too, as currently interpreted, does not obligate the company to adhere exclusively to profitability interests (see Section D IV 1 c, *infra.).* To what extent the change of legal form actually would restrict the execution of a financial institution's public duties can remain an open question, as public functions are guaranteed not on the basis of Article 222 EC Treaty, but rather Article 90,2 EC Treaty.

It is consistent with the fundamental understanding of EU law that public enterprises undertake their commercial activity in accordance with the liberties embodied in the EU Treaty. Article 90 explicitly states that member countries may not undertake or retain any measures relating to public enterprises that contradict the Treaty, particularly Articles 85 through 94. Article 90 EC Treaty is targeted at the member countries and is premised on the principle of equal treatment for private and public enterprises. Specifically to be avoided are situations where public companies achieve a preferential competitive position by appealing to their simultaneous pursuit of public functions.[175] This confirms that the rules governing the performance of public commercial activity are held to be consistent with Article 222 EC Treaty. The EU Commission has the option of effecting this function through appropriate directives or even legal rulings (Article 90,3 EC Treaty). In recent years it has made more frequent use of the judicial process and has severely limited the rights of state enterprises. By way of an

[174] *Rehm,* WM 1993, pp. 133, 138; *cf. Nikolaus Müller,* pp. 464ff., on the difficulties of limiting the profit maximization principle for corporations.

[175] *Pernice* in Grabitz/Hilf, Art. 90, marginal note 1.

example, reference is made merely to the field of telecommunications, where the introduction of open network access has severely limited the possibilities for utilizing public property.[176]

The Commission need not see in Article 222 EC Treaty any sweeping barrier to measures in the context of Article 90 EC Treaty. This restrictive interpretation of the applicability of Article 222 EC Treaty, however, does basically confirm that the liability regulations under discussion here cannot be seen as a subsidy. For in the end, a legal obligation to transform all public companies in the European Union into private limited legal forms under corporate law appears to lie beyond the jurisdiction of EU law. If one concurs with the interpretation of the Commission, then the argument, at least for the legal interpretation developed here, would be that liability regulations that are not supplemental to an already existing liability cannot be considered to be a subsidy within the meaning of Article 92,1 EC Treaty. In other words, under EU law, guarantor liability and institutional burden are not absolutely protected under Article 222 EC Treaty, but neither can they be attacked as subsidies.

IV. Unlimited assumption of liability as common market behavior of a private investor?

It will be examined below whether the current unlimited liability for financial institutions under public law would correspond to the common market behavior of a private investor and whether on this basis there is no subsidy within the meaning of Article 92,1.

In this regard one must first ask whether the conduct of banking business by savings banks and *Landesbanken*, which is related to the fulfillment of special functions, can be understood to represent common market behavior.

Finally, it must be examined whether there are comparable, common forms of assumption of unlimited liability for private banks. This goes directly to the issue of whether a private investor would operate a savings bank in a legal form with unlimited liability.

The standard of comparison is not whether the assumption of unlimited liability in the market could be obtained from unknown third parties. The reference situation is rather to what extent private banks would assume capital and liability obligations for their current or future subsidiaries.

---

[176] *Cf. Pernice,* in Grabitz/Hilf, Art. 90, marginal note 70.

1. The concept of private investor

a) The development of the legal concept of private investor by the Commission and the courts

In order to evaluate financial measures undertaken by the state for the benefit of public enterprises, the Commission applies the principle of the "market-oriented investor". The actions of a private investors are seen as the normal standard for business. Every action undertaken by the state that deviates from this ideal type is categorized as the granting of a subsidy.

In a communiqué of the Commission to member countries it is stated:[177] *"Public enterprises may, under certain circumstances, use their privileged relationship to the state to their advantage if the state makes capital resources available to them under circumstances that go beyond its role as owner. Adherence to the principle of neutrality requires that the difference between the terms under which the state provides resources to the public enterprise and the terms that a private investor would be prepared to offer a private company under normal market conditions, must be considered to be a subsidy."*

The concept of the private investor has been recognized repeatedly by the Court. In one of its most recent decisions it was stated:

" ... that in accordance with an unbroken line of authorities, capital payments of any kind whatsoever made by the state to companies may represent state subsidies if the requirements of Article 92 EWGV are met, and that in order to determine whether such measures are to be construed as state subsidies it must be examined whether a private investor of a size comparable to the public sector administrative institutions would have granted, under similar circumstances, capital assistance of this magnitude." [178]

b) Further development into the "reasonable investor" concept

The practice of the Commission and courts at first simply was oriented toward the self-interest of the hypothetical investor. Important were only

---

[177] OJ. C 273/2 dated 10-18-1991, p. 5.

[178] European Court of Justice dated 10-3-1991, Italy/Commission, Rs. C-261/89, Judgement 1991, I-4437, 4459.

the pecuniary interests of the private investor. This narrow approach has since been abandoned. Additional social and economic aspects are now taken into consideration.

It is recognizeable from the general practice of the Commission that different types of investors must be distinguished from one another. In addition to investors with minority interests, which are characterized by short-term profit maximization and an orientation toward liquidity, the special characteristics of the majority shareholder are considered. A majority shareholder takes a longer-term view and, in addition to profit maximization, pursues other objectives as well, albeit without giving up profitability requirements. A stabile investor of this kind also weighs employment and economic development considerations.

Similar thoughts with respect to the expansion of the private investor concept can be found in the final pleas of Advocate General van Gerven in the "ENI/Lanerossi" decision:[179]

"In a mixed economy in which the interests of the private and public sectors are closely connected and where the interests of employees are emphasized, even a private holding company cannot be completely indifferent to the work force and to the economic development of the region in which it operates."

The European Court followed up on the merits:[180]

"With respect to the behavior of a private investor with which the intervention of a public investor pursuing economic objectives must be compared, it need not necessarily be a matter of the behavior of an average investor who invests capital for the purpose of his more or less short-term profitability, but at the very least a matter of the behavior of a private holding company or a private corporate group that is pursing a global or sectorial structural policy and that is guided by longer-term profitability prospects."

---

[179] Closing arguments of Advocate General *Walter van Gerven* dated 10-11-1990, Rs. 303/88, Italy/Commission, "ENI/Lanerossi", Judgement 1991 I-1451, 1459; similarly Advocate General *van Gerven,* Italy/Commission, "Alfa Romeo", Rs. 305/89, Judgement 1991 I-1625ff.

[180] European Court of Justice dated 3-21-1991, "Alfa Romeo", Rs. 305/89, Judgement 1991 I-1635, 1640 text no. 20; similarly European Court of Justice dated 3-21-1991, Italy/Commission, "ENI/Lanerossi", Judgement 1991 I-1470, 1475, marginal note 18 with respect to regional and social grounds.

c) Additional objectives for consideration in the private investor test

In evaluating possible and permissible objectives of a private enterprise in the context of the private investor text, one must also consider the managerial discretion of the managing board, which is defined under corporate law. One must proceed on the assumption that a permissible entrepreneurial act on the part of the managing board of a corporation – at least under German law – must also be viewed in the context of the private investor test as common market behavior for the state. The managing board of a competing company with private owners (shareholders) has a degree of entrepreneurial discretion in the pursuit of corporate interests that permits consideration of various objectives. This corresponds to the scope of action of the private investor who is generally oriented towards the demands of the market.

Thus in the context of 76 of the German Corporation Law (AktG), it is considered to be well established that the managing board, in its corporate policy, is not obligated to pursue solely the objective of sustained high profits. It certainly lies within the realm of entrepreneurial discretion to consider objectives such as the fair compensation of employees, the arrangement of company working conditions, the social integration of the company, the maintenance of an environment worth living in, and even the demands of the national economy.[181] The fact that the corporation develops a manifold network of social and political contacts and takes part in social, political and cultural activities is a prerequisite for its social acceptance, without which in the long run the commercially successful pursuit of the corporate object cannot be ensured. The participation of the corporation in social life, as is expected or at least sanctioned for enterprises of a similar type and size, thus belongs in the realm of business policy incumbent upon the managing board, the scope of which cannot be curtailed even by corporate by-laws.[182] The Federal Supreme Court ruled as follows in its VEBA decision:

"First, it is not consistent with total reality . . . that public and private economic interests, as the motivating forces behind commercial activity, should be viewed as strict opposites. Public and entrepreneurial concerns,

---

[181] *Mertens,* Kölner Kommentar zum Aktiengesetz, 76, marginal note 11, pp. 32ff.

[182] *Mertens,* Kölner Kommentar zum Aktiengesetz, 76, marginal note 11, 32ff.; *cf. Hefermehl* in *Geßler/Hefermehl,* 58, marginal note 86.

public and private company policies do not exclude each other but may in fact be congruent or at least overlap. Thus on the one hand the obligation of the executive organs of a company with respect to the company's welfare does not preclude their appropriate consideration of national economic perspectives and the common good within the framework of their accountability (93, 116 AktG) and the corporate object set forth in the by-laws." [183]

A bonding of private companies to the social welfare principle can be inferred from this decision of the Federal Consitutional Court concerning worker participation in management.[184]

In management literature as well, it has long been held to be unquestionable that business objectives frequently go beyond the pure maximization of profits, encompassing objectives such as job preservation, worker participation, protection of public health or environmental protection, among others.[185] The pursuit of objectives that go beyond pure profitability considerations is also regularly seen in media companies.

One can assume that companies in private-law form, for example special purpose companies, also frequently disregard a primary orientation towards profitability due to their pursuit of other corporate objectives. This is not true only for companies with non-profit, social or ecological objectives. It is also frequently the case that profitability considerations are placed in the background due to division of labor factors within a group of companies.

The common market behavior of a private investor that is the standard for purposes of defining a subsidy thus goes beyond efforts to maximize short-term profits, and may take into consideration, among other things, social, employment-related or regional policy goals as well.

---

[183] BGH, Decision of 10-13-1977, BGHZ 69, 334 = AG 1978, 50, 52.

[184] BVerfG, Decision of 3-1-1979, NJW 1979, 699.

[185] *Cf. Jung,* Allgemeine Betriebswirtschaftslehre, p. 28; *Körndorfer,* Allgemeine Betriebswirtschaftslehre, 11th edition 1996, pp. 63, 64. In an empirical study conducted by *Raffée/Fritz,* ZfbF 1992, pp. 303, 310, employers highlighted the following corporate objectives: safeguarding the existence of the company, increasing competitive ability, customer satisfaction, long-term profitability, product quality, operating at capacity, growth, increase of sales and productivity, maintaining and creating jobs, market share, employee satisfaction, social responsibility, public reputation, environmental protection.

d) Entrepreneurial discretion of the state

A definitive determination of what is to be considered common market behavior of a private investor is not only problematic with respect to the nature of the various objects worthy of consideration. It is also difficult for a third party to weigh the objectives and to estimate future developments. For entrepreneurial finance or investment decisions, a subjective inclination to take risks plays a decisive role. This is inherent to the individual personality and it cannot be fully equated with entrepreneurial rationality of action.

In light of case practice that to date has been limited to crisis industries, the private investor test has been considered to be generally questionable with respect to profitable companies, because both the financing behavior as well as yield expectations are too manifold to be able to derive clear conclusions from them.[186] In any event, the Commission is not permitted to impose its own opinion in the place of that of the investor. Accordingly, one reads the following in a communiqué of the Commission dated 7-28-1993 on the topic of the entrepreneurial discretion of the state:[187]

"In the event of additional capital needs, public enterprises and public investors, just as private enterprises and private investors, must calculate the risk of and expected return from a planned investment. For its part, the Commission realizes that this risk analysis, for public enterprises just as for private enterprises, requires the application of entrepreneurial abilities and by its very nature entails a wide range of possible judgment criteria on the part of the investor. Within this wide range of possible judgment criteria, the presence of state subsidies cannot be inferred from the investor's decision."

There is thus a wide margin of entrepreneurial discretion with respect to the inclination to take risks or the calculation of risks and the assessment of future developments[188], as well as with respect to the interests that can bear on the considerations. The assessment of a state measure in the context of subsidy supervision must be undertaken on the basis of the information that was available at the time of the measure.[189]

---

[186] *Cf. Schneider/Busch,* EuZW 1995, pp. 602, 608.
[187] Communiqué of the Commission on public companies, text no. 27.
[188] *Hellingman,* CMLR 1986, pp. 111, 119.
[189] *Hellingman,* CMLR 1986, pp. 111, 119.

2. The business operations of savings banks and *Landesbanken* as comparable to the common market behavior of private banks

Private investors pursue numerous objectives in addition to short-term profit maximization and base those objectives on different subjective inclinations towards risk and different expectations. In making use of the wide margin of entrepreneurial discretion that is established thereby, the state can assign certain functions and hence also profitability expectations to savings banks and *Landesbanken*.

One argument against a characterization as common market behavior might be the orientation of public-law financial institutions toward moderate profits rather than maximum profits, if that orientation does not entail profitability prospects; for as can be gathered from precedents of the European Court, common market behavior presupposes long-term profitability prospects.

In general, the banking business in Germany must be viewed as profitable. The healthy, stabile financial results of the banking sector are demonstrated, among other ways, by the high return on liable capital. The ratio of annual profit to liable capital averaged 11.83% for the entire banking sector in 1994.[190]

This high profitability is also fundamentally the case for public-law financial institutions. If one takes the ratio of annual pre-tax surplus to average volume of business as a standard of profitability, then savings banks, with 0.72%, were way over the industry average of 0.47%, and even ahead of the major banks, with 0.58%, in 1994. *Landesbanken* and special-purpose financial institutions as well, with 0.20% and 0.21%[191], respectively, must be considered as profitable enterprises. In assessing these figures one must take into consideration that *Landesbanken*, which have no access to lucrative retail banking, work in conjunction with savings banks in an arrangement based on the division of labor.

Still, it is conceivable, and has actually occurred in isolated instances, that financial institutions under public law incur losses. To the extent that these losses are caused by the special functions assigned to public banks, it could be asked whether the operation of these banks might nevertheless be seen

---

[190] *Cf.* Deutsche Bundesbank Monatsbericht, October 1995, p. 21.

[191] *Cf.* Deutsche Bundesbank Monatsbericht, October 1995, p. 37.

as common market behavior. From the perspective of their sacrifice of potentially higher profits as well, it is questionable to what extent the objectives pursued by public financial institutions are compatible with the objectives of a market oriented investor.

It was determined above that the common market behavior of a "reasonable investor", which is used as a standard for determining a subsidy, goes beyond an effort to attain short-term profitability and encompasses, among other things, social, structural or regional policy objectives, allowing for a wide margin of entrepreneurial discretion.

As a rule, the public mandate of savings banks and *Landesbanken* is fulfilled efficiently. This is also in accordance with statutory requirements for efficient management. The business of these institutions would also be seen as common for the market even without a demonstration of current profits if at the very least there are prospects for medium-term profits. As long as public-law financial institutions are not without long-term profitability prospects, common market behavior must be assumed, for the range of assessment options for entrepreneurial decisions of public authorities also encompasses the special functions of savings banks and *Landesbanken*.

The objective of adequately supplying the population with banking services must not be understood as being contrary to entrepreneurial objectives simply because it is not in keeping with short-term profit maximization. Accepting savings deposits from everyone and making current accounts widely available in the context of savings banks' supply function can also serve to promote the image and social acceptance of an enterprise, i.e. of a savings bank. In so doing, savings banks ensure the continued existence of their enterprise and, indirectly, also promote the long-term realization of profits.

The operation of savings banks and *Landesbanken* must therefore be understood as the common market behavior of a private investor, comparable to that of private banks.[192]

---

[192] *Cf.* also *Scherer/Schödermeier*, ZBB 1996, pp. 165, 175.

3. The assumption of unlimited liability for savings banks and *Landesbanken* as common market behavior of a private investor

For the questions that are to be investigated here, it is of decisive importance for the application of the private investor test to determine whether private investors also conduct banking transactions in a form that leads to an obligation comparable to guarantor liability and institutional burden.

a) Forms of unlimited assumption of liability in banking transactions

aa) Establishment and acquisition of private companies

Private banks in Germany are operated in widely different legal forms. Whereas the largest and most well-known banks conduct their business as corporations, there is also a number of private banks in the legal form of private partnerships (OHG), limited partnerships (KG) or partnerships limited by shares (KGaA). Examples include *Sal. Oppenheim & Cie. KGaA, M.M. Warburg & Co., Merck, Finck & Co., Trinkaus & Burkhardt KGaA.*

For some private banks, the natural persons present as fully liable partners at the time of foundation are later replaced by legal persons, particularly major banks as corporations. But there are also a considerable number of private banks for which private persons as partners of a private partnership or as unlimited partners of a limited partnership are personally fully liable partners pursuant to 128 HGB). According to bank statistics of the Central Bank of Germany, 67 so-called "private bankers", *i.e.* financial institutions in the legal form of a sole trader or a private partnership, showed a total business volume of DM 52,4 billion in 1995.[193]

Both establishing as well as joining a bank operated as a private partnership entails the free decision of a natural or legal person to risk that person's entire personal assets without limitation of liability for purposes of conducting banking transactions. The assumption of unlimited liability is common for private partnerships in the private banking sector.

---

[193] Deutsche Bundesbank Monatsbericht, October 1995, statistical portion, p. 20.

bb) Comfort letters

A comfort letter to creditors contains a parent company's pledge to supply a subsidiary with the financial resources required for the subsidiary to meet its obligations.

There are different practical and legal forms that such a letter can take. The comfort letter is not an established legal concept, but rather a collective term for everything from simple letters of intent with the character of goodwill to obligations with more of a surety-like or guarantee-like quality.[194]

One must distinguish fundamentally between "hard" and "soft" comfort letters. The latter are non-binding letters of intent, given without a desire for their being legally binding, that hold out the prospect of a certain business or investment policy on the part of the parent company.

The "classic" hard comfort letter reads: *"We will ensure that, until the loan is fully repaid, our subsidiary is endowed such that it is able at any time to meet its obligations in connection with the loan."* [195]

A "hard" comfort letter is understood to be a unilaterally binding contract *sui generis*[196], in which the endowment obligation with respect to the subsidiary takes the form of an artificial non-genuine contract for the benefit of a third party.[197] The claim of performance thereunder is that the parent company would supply sufficient funds to the subsidiary so that the subsidiary is able to pay back its obligations; the parent company bears the "forwarding risk".[198] The comfort letter thus does not form the basis for a primary claim on the part of the creditors. However, it is recognized that a violation of the comfort letter gives rise to secondary claims for damages against the parent company.[199] Fault on the part of the parent company is not a prerequisite for the damages claim.[200]

---

[194] *Michalski,* WM 1994, pp. 1229, 1230, with additional references; *Habersack,* ZIP 1996, p. 257; for a general discussion of comfort letters, *cf.* BGHZ 117, 127, 130 = WM 1992, p. 501.

[195] *Cf. Michalski,* WM 1994, pp. 1229, 1234, with numerous examples for the formulation of hard comfort letters.

[196] *Stecher,* p. 81; *Michalski,* WM 1994, pp. 1229, 1232.

[197] Probably a unanimous opinion *Stecher,* p. 81; *Michalski,* WM 1994, pp. 1229, 1238; *Habersack,* ZIP 1996, pp. 257, 258.

[198] *Cf. Michalski,* WM 1994, pp. 1229, 1238.

[199] *Cf. Michalski,* WM 1994, p. 1229; U.H. *Schneider,* ZIP 1989, p. 619; *Habersack,* ZIP 1996, pp. 257, 263.

[200] *Cf. Kohut,* Patronatserklärungen, 1984, p. 185; *Michalski,* WM 1994, pp. 1229, 1240.

The comfort letter for the benefit of a subsidiary is issued not only in order to improve the subsidiary's creditworthiness. The general financial soundness so critically important to the business life of a company that is to be given a big contract can also be ensured by means of a comfort letter. By means of a comfort letter, the principal receives the security that the company will be able to handle the large order financially, and thus the completion of the order is ensured.[201]

Comfort letters from parent financial institutions to creditors of their subsidiary banks are common practice in the banking industry. They are given both from a long-term perspective within the "normal" course of business as well as in actual crisis situations of the subsidiary.

Comfort letters to the general public are issued specifically in the annual reports of the major private banks.[202] For example, in the appendix to the financial statements in Deutsche Bank's 1994 annual report it is stated: "Deutsche Bank AG ensures, except for cases of political risk, that the following banks and their affiliates can fulfill their contractual obligations."[203]

One must proceed on the assumption that such letters directed at all creditors give rise to the right to assert damage claims against the parent company.[204]

---

[201] *Cf.* Higher Regional Court (OLG) of Dusseldorf WM 1989, p. 1842; *Michalski,* WM 1994, p. 1229.

[202] On the annual reports of Deutsche Bank and Dresdner Bank, *Cf. Schneider/Busch,* EuZW 1995, pp. 602, 607; extensive treatment in *U.H. Schneider,* ZIP 1989, pp. 619ff.

[203] Annual Report of Deutsche Bank AG for 1994, p. 79. A similar obligation can be found in annual reports of Dresdner Bank AG, e.g. for the year 1988, p. 83: "For group companies that are subject to our uniform management and that undertake banking or banking-related functions, we ensure, apart from cases of political risk and in the context of our participating interest, that they can meet their contractual obligations."

[204] *Habersack* ZIP 1996, pp. 257, 160, derives this from the accounting practice with respect to contingent liabilities. A legal contractual commitment on the part of the bank making the comfort letter is also assumed in *U.H. Schneider,* ZIP 1989, pp. 619, 624, as well in Festschrift für *Krümmel,* pp. 351, 361; taking a different view only *Larenz/Canaris* Schuldrecht II/2, 60 V 2 d, p. 84.

The Deposit Guarantee Fund of the Federal Association of German Banks obligates its member institutions, through 5,10 of the statutes, to indemnify the fund by issuing comfort letters for the benefit of the respective subsidiaries.[205]

Comfort letters are also required by the bank supervision authorities in Great Britain and Luxembourg from the parent banks of banks operating in those countries.[206]

cc) Covenants to cover losses

In contrast to a comfort letter, which in terms of liability law effects the external relationship between creditor and parent company, a covenant to cover losses creates an internal relationship between parent company and subsidiary. A covenant to cover losses establishes an obligation on the part of the parent company with respect to the subsidiary to supply the subsidiary with the financial resources required for it to meet its obligations.[207]

dd) Right of recourse of the Deposit Guarantee Fund against the parent company

In the event of the failure of a member bank, the Deposit Guarantee Fund of the Federal Association of German Banks provides for a right of legal recourse of the fund against any existing parent bank for the obligations of the subsidiary that were paid from the fund.[208]

For the parent bank this means that the decision to join the Deposit Guarantee Fund implies full liability for obligations of the subsidiary bank secured by the fund.

---

[205] *Cf. U.H. Schneider,* ZIP 1989, p. 619.

[206] *U.H. Schneider,* ZIP 1989, p. 619; *Wagner,* p. 25.

[207] *Cf. Karsten Schmidt,* Festschrift *Werner,* 1984, p. 777ff.; *Schneider/Busch,* EuZW 1995, p. 602, 607.

[208] § 5,10 of the By-Laws, *cf. Schneider/Busch,* EuZW 1995, pp. 602, 607; U.H. *Schneider,* ZIP 1989, p. 619.

b) Assumption of liability under private law in comparison with guarantor liability and institutional burden

Private banks assume a voluntary unlimited liability for future obligations of their subsidiaries by means of comfort letters and covenants to cover losses, and also by means of shareholder liability at the time of founding or joining a private partnership. Joining the Deposit Guarantee Fund, too, can be understood as a voluntary assumption of liability for the deposit obligations of the subsidiary bank vis-a-vis non-banks. Article 2362 of the Italian civil code provides for unlimited liability for all obligations in the event all shares of a company are purchased, regardless of the legal form.[209]

Comfort letters establish rights to secondary damages claims on the part of creditors against the parent company. Thus, as is the case for guarantor liability, they relate to the external relationship.[210]

A covenant to cover losses, on the other hand, relates to the internal relationship, and thus in this respect is more similar to institutional burden. Since guarantor liability and institutional burden are inextricably connected to one another and have a graduated relationship, both of these institutions are treated as one and the same.

aa) Liability for all obligations with respect to all creditors

Guarantor liability is directed at all creditors of an institution. Comfort letters are frequently issued in the annual reports of banks. To this extent they are directed at all creditors of a subsidiary. To the extent that covenants to cover losses indirectly serve to satisfy the creditors of a subsidiary, this applies equally to all creditors of the subsidiary. Shareholder liability, pursuant to 128 HGB also exists with respect to all creditors of a subsidiary that is in the legal form of a private partnership.

Comfort letters, covenants to cover losses and shareholder liability, just as guarantor liability, thus encompass all obligations of a subsidiary or institution, as the case may be, and do not merely secure individual obligations.

---

[209] *Cf.* Communiqué of the Commission pursuant to Article 93,2 EU Treaty to the remaining member countries and other interested parties concerning a subsidization plan of Italy for the benefit of EFIM, OJ. C 349/2 dated 12-29-1993, p. 3.

[210] *U.H. Schneider*, DB 1992, pp. 769, 773.

bb) Secondary liability

Guarantor liability is subsidiary. Similarly, an obligation to pay damages based on a comfort letter arises only following an attempted claim against the subsidiary. Only under this condition do creditors have a claim against a parent company for the financial endowment of a subsidiary.

Shareholder liability pursuant to 128 HGB is fundamentally a direct, non-subordinate liability on the part of shareholders. In the context of proper corporate financing, however, there is, as a rule, sufficient capital, which in an emergency can be supplemented by an additional contribution to the company within the internal relationship in order to prevent a disruption of business operations. The contribution of liable capital from partners of a private partnership or from unlimited partners in the context of reasonable and proper corporate financing corresponds to the required actions of the founding body and guarantor with respect to savings banks and *Landesbanken,* respectively.

As does institutional burden, a covenant to cover losses relates to the financing obligation of a parent company for its subsidiary.

The actual form of shareholder liability, comfort letters and covenants to cover losses corresponds to institutional burden (which virtually alone is relevant) as financing within the internal relationship. The obligation of the founder of the institution to keep it functional is thus comparable to the voluntary assumption of liability by private banks in the aforementioned forms.

There is a parallel between the financing laws for public and private banks.[211]

cc) Preliminary conclusion

The state's assumption of risk established by guarantor liability and institutional burden corresponds to the forms of voluntary assumption of liability for private banks, because it entails comprehensive liability for all obligations to all creditors of the subsidiary, and in practice is characterized by a contribution of capital within the internal relationship (priority of institutional burden).

---

211 *Schneider/Busch,* EuZW 1995, pp. 602, 605; *Scherer/Schödermeier,* ZBB 1996, pp. 165, 177; *Gruson/Schneider,* CBLR 1995, pp. 337, 425.

The decision of the public authorities to operate savings banks and *Landesbanken* as independent institutions with institutional burden and guarantor liability ensues within the framework of the state's permissible organizational discretion in the selection of legal form[212] and, considering the fundamentally broad discretion in the context of the private investor test[213], it must be understood as the common market behavior of a private investor.

According to the understanding of the private investor test, it does not matter whether a capital transfer or the assumption of liability is associated with corporate control.[214] According to legal precedents of the European Court, what is decisive is whether there is a reasonable expectation on the part of the investor for achieving a profit. This is not tied to control rights in the company.

c) No comparability due to the immeasurable financial resources of the state?

In the opinion of *Koenig*[215], guarantor liability is not comparable to liability structures in the private banking sector. He asserts that the latter are backed by a fixed and limited amount of capital and ultimately a default risk. Institutional burden and guarantor liability for a savings bank or *Landesbank,* on the other hand, are backed, as it has been expressed by the Commission in the "EFIM" decision[216], by the "immeasurable financial resources" of the state, and hence by its virtually absolute credit solvency. *Koenig* argues that credit solvency of this kind is not achievable on the private market. For him the more decisive difference is that comfort letters or covenants to cover losses, unlike institutional burden and guarantor liability, which are established by law, are based on a limited capital ceiling, so that the market comparison loses its impact.

---

[212] See Section B III 3, *supra.*

[213] *Cf.* Section D IV 1, *supra.*

[214] This is the tendency of *Gleske,* p. 338.

[215] *Koenig,* EuZW 1995, pp. 595, 600.

[216] Communiqué of the Commission pursuant to Article 93,2 EU Treaty to member countries and other interested parties concerning a subsidization plan of Italy for the benefit of EFIM, OJ. C 349/2 dated 12-29-1993, p. 3.

The argument that "such credit solvency is not achievable on the private market" cannot have a bearing on the subsidy discussion. Several private banks active in the capital markets in Germany enjoy a better standing than most public-law banks. For example, in Germany there is not a single public-law bank that has a better credit rating than *Deutsche Bank.* For the application of subsidy law to state guarantees for public banks one must also take care that the creditworthiness of some states is rated lower than some private companies in those states[217] or other member countries.[218]

Thus for public companies in general one cannot speak of the "immeasurable financial resources" of the state and of a virtually absolute credit solvency.[219]

Further, it is questionable to what extent the liability of the "immeasurable financial resources" of the state are limited to the public banks with guarantor liability. The support of *Crédit Lyonnais* by the French government[220] – which was declared to be unobjectionable in terms of subsidy law – the *Banesto* case in Spain[221] and the *Banco di Napoli* case in Italy[222], as well as the bank crises in Scandinavia and in Japan all document that in most countries there is de facto state liability for major banks under the principle of "too big to fail."[223] In light of this de facto state liability, one can no longer speak of there being a limitation of liability for private banks based on the aforementioned "limited capital ceiling."

Based on recent precedents of the Commission it is doubtful whether public companies in fact can fall back on unlimited state resources.

---

[217] Here, however, attention must be paid to the so-called "sovereign ceiling" for the rating, whereby the credit solvency of the home country and hence the country-related risk represents the upper limit for the rating of a company, *cf. Everling,* Credit Rating durch internationale Agenturen, p. 140; on ratings, see Section E III 3, *infra.*

[218] *Cf.* also *Scherer/Schödermeier,* ZBB 1996, pp. 165, 177.

[219] *Cf. Schneider/Busch,* EuZW 1995, pp. 602, 608.

[220] *Cf.* Section G II 1, *infra.*

[221] *Cf.* Section G II 2, *infra.*

[222] At the end of March 1996 the Italian government undertook a rescue operation for the seventh-largest Italian bank, *Banco di Napoli,* whereby the equivalent of DM 1.9 billion was paid by the state directly to the bank, *cf.* Handelsblatt dated 3-28-1996, p. 25.

[223] *Cf.* Section B IV 4, *supra.*

In the EFIM decision, the Commission considered the issue of a guarantee by the Italian government for all obligations of a company. This guarantee was based on Article 2362 of the Italian civil code, which establishes unlimited liability for all obligations of wholly-owned subsidiaries. The Commission commented as follows:[224]

"The guaranteeing of all debts of a company is an act that a market-oriented investor would not undertake without making sure that the additional risk is offset by additional profits. . . .
Further, a market-oriented shareholder would restrict this 'unlimited' liability by liquidating an enterprise as soon as he has reason to fear that his debts have exceeded the value of his assets and that this is not merely a momentary decline in value."

The Commission decided that the guarantee and assumption of liability of the state-owned holding company EFIM and its wholly-owned subsidiary must be seen as a subsidy. They further stated:

"Upon expiration of the term provided for in the agreement, Article 2362 is only applicable to public enterprises in those cases that are comparable to cases that would be acceptable to a market-oriented investor. From this point in time forward, all creditors will be able to assess and estimate the credit-worthiness of public companies only in terms of the companies' net worth."[225]

If one applies the criteria of the Commission's EFIM decision to institutional burden and guarantor liability, then this means that the unlimited liability of the state is only consistent with subsidy law and thus only legally valid if the benefitting company can pass the private investor test, *i.e.* operates profitably. However, if the state can only make use of its financial resources as a private investor would do, then the resources that are usable for the execution of institutional burden are also limited.[226]

To this extent, neither can the credit solvency of the guarantor be of any importance for purposes of subsidy control. Subsidy control is behavior

---

[224] Communiqué of the Commission pursuant to Article 93,2 EC Treaty to the remaining member countries and the other interested parties concerning a subsidization plan of Italy for the benefit of EFIM, OJ. C 349/2 dated 12-29-1993, p. 4.

[225] EFIM decision, *loc. cit.*, p. 6.

[226] *Schneider/Busch,* EuZW 1995, pp. 602, 608.

control. The behavior of a market-oriented investor has no bearing on the credit solvency of the liable party.[227]

The state's liability is undoubtedly associated in many cases with high credit solvency. The question of whether a possibly connected improvement in refinancing terms represents a subsidy is discussed separately below. However, the credit solvency of the state does not stand in the way of the fundamental comparability of guarantor liability and the assumption of liability under private law.

d) Preliminary conclusion

In conclusion it can be said that covenants to cover losses, comfort letters and shareholder liability represent possible methods for the assumption of liability for private banks and that in practice they are indeed customary. Institutional burden and guarantor liability are fundamentally comparable to them. In making a – hypothetical – decision to operate a savings bank or *Landesbank* and to furnish either with guarantor liability, the state is acting within the limits of the private investor test. The provision of public-law financial institutions with unlimited liability within the framework of institutional burden and guarantor liability must be seen as the common market behavior of a private investor and to this extent does not represent a subsidy.

There can only be preferential treatment of public enterprises by means of an unlimited state liability if a reasonable private investor, due to the completely hopeless financial results of the financial institution, would not issue a letter of support and would choose to liquidate the financial institution. Thus there is only a subsidy if guarantor liability and institutional burden are retained even though a comparable private investor would have restricted or terminated this unlimited liability.

The use of institutional burden and guarantor liability is therefore basically possible and permissible. Only on an individual basis, in a case where there is no prospect of long-term profitability, does an obligation to liquidate or terminate liability arise.[228]

---

[227] *Cf. Schneider/Busch,* EuZW 1995, pp. 602, 608; *Scherer/Schödermeier,* ZBB 1996, pp. 165, 177.

[228] *Cf.* also Section F, *infra.*

V. Institutional burden and guarantor liability as the expression of financing responsibility under corporate law

The subsidy supervision of the Commission seeks to treat private and public companies in accordance with the principle of neutrality.[229] To the extent that institutional burden and guarantor liability are in accordance with financing law and liability regulations for private companies, then the principle of equal treatment of public and private companies cannot be violated by these institutions.

German corporation law does not provide for a comprehensive system of preventive creditor protection through the vehicle of an effective capital contribution requirement. Through legal precedents and later also through legislation, a restrictive legal protection was created for creditors. The shareholders are made responsible for a lack of liable capital, *i.e.* undercapitalization.[230] This has been characterized by the Federal Supreme Court as a transition to financing responsibility.[231]

Undercapitalization exists under the terms of corporate limited liability when the liable capital is not sufficient to cover the existing medium-term or long-term need for capital – depending on the nature and scope of the desired or actual business activity, and with a view to the actual financing methods – that cannot be covered by loans from third parties.[232] Thus a distinguishing characteristic is the incongruity between liable capital and the corporate objective. One must distinguish between a nominal undercapitalization and a material undercapitalization. If at least loans or economically equal services were supplied, one speaks of a nominal undercapitalization. If capital contributions by shareholders are altogether absent, or if they are insufficient, then it is a matter of a material undercapitalization.

The nominal undercapitalization, covered by shareholder loans replacing the liable capital and by other means comparable to the extension of loans, is the subject of §§ 32a, 32b of the Limited Liability Company Act (GmbHG). Even if these regulations do not establish a contribution

---

229 OJ. C 273/2 dated 10-18-1991, p. 5.

230 *Wüst*, JZ 1995, pp. 990, 992.

231 BGH, 9-19-1988, BGHZ 105, 168, 176.

232 *Cf. Goerdeler/Müller* in *Hachenberg/Ulmer*, GmbH, appendix to 30, marginal note 16.

requirement for shareholders, they do at the very least equate the capital borrowed from the shareholders with the liable capital. Loans extended in a crisis are treated as quasi liable capital and cannot be demanded back in the event of bankruptcy.

For material undercapitalization, which is not regulated by law, legal precedents and literature recognize a liability on the part of shareholders as a matter of principle. The personably liable shareholders or sole shareholder of a GmbH is made subject to liability if the actual capitalization of the company is not in keeping with the company's objective. In addition to a claim based on 826 of the German Civil Code (BGB), various forms of extended recourse and a good faith liability are under discussion.[233] In exceptional cases, extended recourse has been accepted by the Federal Supreme Court.[234] Even if the dogmatic requirements and consequences of this type of liability are disputed, there still remains a broad consensus concerning the recognition of the extension of liability beyond the legal person.[235]

These principles are applicable to savings banks and *Landesbanken.* If savings banks or *Landesbanken* are not sufficiently capitalized by their guarantor, then under corporation law, too, recourse by the creditors to the guarantors would be possible.

To this extent the principle under corporation law of an adequate capitalization, *i.e.* of financing responsibility, corresponds to the public-law right of financing through guarantor liability and institutional burden.

Corporate group liability pursuant to §§ 302, 303 AktG presents a certain parallel to institutional burden and guarantor liability. Here one must take into consideration that the state can also be seen as a controlling company within the meaning of group company law.[236] By means of a control agreement or a profit transfer agreement, the controlling company is obligated under 302 AktG to offset the annual deficit of a dependent company. This obligation does not directly lead to an external liability towards creditors of the controlling company. Pursuant to the code of civil procedure, creditors

---

[233] *Cf.* evidence cited in *Wüst,* JZ 1995, pp. 990, 994.

[234] BGH dated 7-8-1970, BGHZ 54, 222, „Siedlerfall".

[235] *Cf. Blaurock,* Festschrift *Stimpel,* 1985, pp. 553, 559; *Wüst,* JZ 1995, pp. 990, 993ff.; *Stimpel,* Festschrift Goerdeler, pp. 601ff.; *Karsten Schmidt,* Gesellschaftsrecht, pp. 205ff., *Karsten Schmidt,* JZ 1985, pp. 301, 302; *Raiser,* pp. 335, 336.

[236] *Cf.,* among others, the VEBA decision, BGHZ 69, 334.

can attach a claim asserted against the dependent company to the controlling company and can effect payment.[237] This rule demonstrates proximity to institutional burden. It shows that a shareholder, whose position is comparable to the sovereign bearing financial responsibility for a legally independent public institution, may be obligated to assume personal liability even under conditions of limited liability.

In conclusion, there is in corporation law a tendency to privilege creditor protection over an absolute limitation on capital contributions and thus over the interests of shareholders. If the associated principle of proper corporate financing is violated, this can lead to the liability of the shareholders beyond the specific amount of the shareholder's stake in the company's capital stock. The principle of financing responsibility is comparable to the financing regulations under public law by means of guarantor liability and institutional liability. Further, these obligations can be seen as an element of creditor protection under group company law. Guarantor liability and institutional burden thereby correspond to company-law institutions of creditor protection that lead to a responsibility on the part of shareholders, even in a limited liability legal form.

This means that in choosing a private legal form for savings banks and *Landesbanken*, there could very well be financial recourse against the previous guarantors. This could not be understood as a subsidy.

The permissibility under corporation law of a direct, unlimited liability on the part of the state also follows from the new corporate transformation laws. Pursuant to § 301,2 of the Transformation Act (UmwG), a public-law corporation or institution can become a stock corporation by changing its legal form. It follows from § 303,1 UmwG that a transformation into a partnership limited by shares is also possible. However, to do so requires the approval of all shareholders who would have the position of personally liable shareholders in the new company. It follows directly from this that the state may act as personally liable partner in a partnership limited by shares (KGaA). Contrary to the institutions under corporation law discussed above, this is not a matter of the extension of liability to shareholders, but rather their direct responsibility under liability law.

---

[237] *Cf. Hüffer,* AktG, § 302, marginal note 18.

E. Institutional burden and guarantor liability as subsidies by virtue of refinancing advantages?

Guarantor liability and institutional burden, as liability by virtue of organization, are not subject to subsidy control. Thus for subsidy control as behavior control, the credit solvency of the guarantor is fundamentally irrelevant.

Guarantor liability and institutional burden are attributed with an improvement of creditworthiness or of "potential outside financing capacity." More favorable refinancing terms for public banks could be associated with this. This benefit can be understood as a subsidy. A characterization of this kind must be clearly distinguished from the previously discussed issue of whether guarantor liability and institutional burden as such may be ascribed to the factual conditions of Article 92,1 EC Treaty. A benefit by means of refinancing terms would be an additional element, causally related to guarantor liability and institutional burden.

I. Presence of an economic benefit

1. Reduction of refinancing costs through institutional burden and guarantor liability

In a communiqué to the member countries dated November 1993, the Commission expressed the following view:[238]

"38.1. Public companies whose by-laws preclude bankruptcy are virtually in possession of a standing subsidy (synonymous with a surety) ***for all loans,*** *if the by-laws permit the companies in question to take out loans under more favorable terms than would otherwise be granted them; in such cases the same principles must be applied.*

38.2. If the participation of the state in a public company is associated with unlimited liability rather than the usual limitation of liability, then the Commission will treat this as a surety ***for all funds*** *that are subject to unlimited liability. In this case the principles discussed above are applicable to the guarantee."*

---

[238] Communiqué of the Commission on public companies, text no. 38.1; *cf.* text no. 3 with respect to the applicability of the report outside of the manufacturing industry.

In the draft report dated 3-7-1995 to member countries concerning the application of Articles 92 and 93 EC Treaty to state subsidies that are granted in the form of sureties, it is written:

"2.9. The Commission draws attention to the fact that it takes the position that more favorable terms for loans that state companies have received whose status precludes the possibility of bankruptcy represent a subsidy in the form of a surety; this also holds true with respect to the participation of the state in a company if that participation is associated with unlimited rather than the usual limited liability."

The Commission sees the subsidy element of guarantees in the

"difference between the interest rate that the borrower would pay on the free market and the actual rate paid as a result of the surety, minus the premium paid for the sureties."[239]

The preclusion of bankruptcy for public enterprises that is associated with guarantor liability and institutional burden, as was argued above, cannot be equated with a state surety. This is contrary to the position of the Commission. It can have the effect of a surety, however, as far as its significance for raising capital is concerned.

It must be assumed that by means of guarantor liability and institutional burden of the state the risk of an investment in a public bank in the Federal Republic is considered to be relatively low. Since reduced risks are normally less rewarding on the market, a lower interest rate and associated lower refinancing costs are obvious for public banks.[240]

It must be examined whether and in what cases one can assume an improvement of refinancing conditions as a result of the liability of the state,

---

[239] Communiqué of the Commission, see previous footnote, text no. 38.

[240] An improvement of the credit rating for *Landesbanken,* which frequently is equated with an improvement in refinancing terms, is in principle not doubted in legal literature; *cf.* among others *Thode,* Sparkasse 1994, pp. 134, 136; *Dörries,* Zur Rechtsstellung von *Landesbanken* unter besonderer Berücksichtigung der Westdeutschen Landesbank, 1988, pp. 114ff.; *Koenig,* EuZW 1995, p. 595; *Schneider/Busch* EuZW 1995, pp. 602, 608; *Dennig,* Wirtschaftsdienst 1995, pp. 210, 214. *Rehm,* WM 1993, 133, 136 points to the impact of a privatization of *Landesbanken* on their credit rating. *Möschel,* Festschrift Raisch, p. 481, and *Seidel,* EG-Binnenmarkt und öffentliche Unternehmen, pp. 343, 350, derive from this the subsidy-like character of guarantor liability.

whether a benefit of this kind can be established with sufficient certainty, and to what extent it can be quantified.

2. No benefit to public banks due to a de facto liability on the part of the state for all major banks

One could call into question the assumption of there being a benefit for public banks over private banks because there would appear to be a de facto state liability or guarantee for the continued existence of major financial institutions in all member countries.[241]

In Germany, one could agree that there is a guarantee of the function and existence of larger financial institutions, at least with respect to the major private banks.[242] The support by the French government of *Crédit Lyonnais*, which at the time was the largest financial institution in Europe, illustrates the de facto recognition of the principle "too big to fail."

The consideration of the credit solvency of the home country does not take place only with respect to public banks. The creditworthiness of private banks is also influenced by the country-related risk. This is also illustrated by the fact that in assigning a rating[243] to bonds of private banks, the country-related risk is a contributing factor.[244] The hypothetical disregard of the state's credit solvency in the stand-alone rating and the legal rating of IBCA seems to support this view.[245] An argument for the absence of a benefit cannot be based on this line of reasoning, because the merely de facto or economic guarantee for private banks has a different intensity than the legal guarantee for public banks. Nevertheless, the trust that investors have in the ultimate state support of certain private banks would appear to give rise to a – possibly quantifiable – financing advantage that would seem likely to reduce the extent of any existing benefit for public banks.

3. No benefit because of simultaneous financing disadvantages?

The chosen legal form and the associated liability of the state are not only associated with advantages in raising capital. The cost of borrowed capital with respect to bonds in fact might be reduced. But on the other hand public

[241] *Cf.* Section B IV 4, *supra;* Section G II, *infra.*

[242] *Cf.* Section B IV 4, *supra.*

[243] The rating of loans is discussed in detail in Section E III 3.

[244] *Cf. Everling,* Der langfristige Kredit 1991, 384; *Ebenroth/Daum,* WM 1992, supplement 5, pp. 1, 4.

[245] On the stand-alone rating and legal rating, *cf.* Section E III 3, *infra.*

banks, as to liable capital and similar financing instruments, do not have access to financing options that are comparable to those of private banks or banking credit cooperatives.

Public financial institutions, by virtue of their legal form, must rely for all intents and purposes on the financial assistance of the founding body for the contribution of liquid core capital. They do not have access to stock exchange trading as a means of raising capital. Thus the potential of the national and international capital markets – which frequently pay high premiums for the issuance of securities – is not available to public banks. Rather these institutions must resort to self-financing or to contributions from local authorities and states, which as a rule have limited financial resources, as the primary means of raising capital.

In calculating the liable capital in the context of state supervision of financial institutions, no additional amount is granted for guarantor liability. The EU Directive and German legislators do not recognize guarantor liability and institutional burden as a "security" in the context of bank supervision.[246] By contrast, for cooperative banks and, upon petition, for the liable partners of private banks, the uncalled liability of the members and the proven free private assets, respectively, are recognized as "liable capital", and pursuant to 10,2 no. 3 and 6 KWG, an additional amount is assessed.

Another structurally determined refinancing disadvantage for *Landesbanken* lies in the fact that *Landesbanken,* due to their corporate structure, cannot avail themselves of favorable refinancing terms via investment in private retail banking.

If, contrary to the view expressed here, one were to see the legal form per se as a benefit within the meaning of subsidy law, then along with the advantages associated with the legal form, one would also have to take into consideration the disadvantages associated with certain forms of refinancing (*cf.* Section B IV 2, *supra*). To this extent, financing facilitation in the form of guarantor liability could be seen as "compensation" for the structural disadvantages of savings banks and *Landesbanken* in other financing areas and with respect to statutory capitalization requirements.[247]

[246] This was affirmed by the Federal Constitutional Court, *cf.* Section B IV 2, *supra.*

[247] *Cf. Rehm,* WM 1993, 133, 134, on the competitive disadvantages of public-law financial institutions caused by the non-recognition of guarantor liability and by more stringent control by the public.

4. Reduction of possible refinancing advantages through bank supervision and guarantee of deposits

As early as 1968, in the government's report on distortions of competition in the credit business and on the guarantee of deposits, it was determined that although public liability did give rise to objective advantages, it was increasingly losing its competitive relevance due to the general supervision of financial institution functioning as a safeguard for institutions and deposits in the broadest sense.[248]

If one takes into consideration the further development of bank supervision and the voluntary safeguarding institutions within the banking sector that have since come into existence, then an even further loss of significance of guarantor liability and institutional burden can be assumed.

II. The assumption of unlimited liability as a common market form of financing for a private investor

To the extent that one accepts the premise of an economic benefit, relevant in terms of subsidy law, for financial institutions under public law as the result of refinancing advantages, that alone would not be sufficient to qualify guarantor liability as a subsidy within the meaning of Art. 92, EC Treaty.

It would further be necessary to examine the subsidy qualification arising out of refinancing advantages within the framework of the private investor test. According to this test, it is crucial whether a private bank or a private holding company also would improve the financing options for its subsidiary bank by assuming unlimited liability.

As to the question of whether a private investor would assume unlimited liability for a savings bank or a Landesbank in order to improve its financing, it also depends, in addition to the generally existing profitability prospects of these institutions[249], on whether a private investor, too, would prefer unlimited liability to a direct payment of capital to the bank.

---

[248] Wettbewerbsenquête, BT-Drucks. V/3500, p. 49.

[249] See Section D IV 2, *supra.*

In this regard for purposes of assessing the common market behavior of the state, it does not matter whether, and under what conditions, a public company can obtain an assumption of liability from a third party. At issue here is rather the behavior of an investor, *i.e.* of a current or potential shareholder, and not to which third party under what terms a bank is granting credits or sureties.

1. Possible means of financing for private enterprises

Private companies and partners have a large number of financing options at their disposal for their subsidiaries in the area of liable capital or capital from outside sources.[250]

On the one hand, financing can be obtained through an increase in liable capital, whereby debts owed by the subsidiary are transformed into liable capital or additional capital is contributed.

The extension of a shareholder loan to the subsidiary lies on a middle ground between outside capital and an increase of liable capital.[251]

Frequently the contribution of capital from outside sources or, as the case may be, the improvement of the financing situation does not occur as the result of a payment by the partners of liable capital or outside capital, but rather as the result of borrowing from outside sources being made easier through the provision of guarantees.

This securing of loans extended by third parties may be limited to individual obligations through sureties or other guarantees, or it can occur in the form of an assumption of unlimited total liability.

An indirect financing of this kind, to the extent it is undertaken in a crisis situation, is the subject of §§ 32a,2, 32b GmbHG. Pursuant thereto, in the event of the bankruptcy of a GmbH, the securitization given by a partner for a loan that was extended by a third party is treated like a contribution of liable capital.

The influence of the assumption of liability on the financing costs is documented by the founding of credit guarantee associations in the 1950s.[252]

---

[250] On the subject of freedom of choice among various financing methods, see *Soukup*, Zogö 1995, pp. 16, 20; *Hellingman*, CMLR 1986, pp. 111, 116.

[251] *Cf.* 32a GmbHG, according to which under certain conditions corporate loans in lieu of owners' equity are treated in a crisis like debts of subsequent rank.

[252] *Cf. Strombeck*, Die Bank 1995, p. 80.

In principle, a private company has the freedom to choose any of the aforementioned self-financing or third-party financing options. Apart from the provisions of company law and bank supervision law, a private company or private bank makes decisions concerning the form of financing based on cost and profitability considerations.

The assumption of liability can very well be profitable, particularly from the perspective of liquidity, as against a direct contribution of capital. Frequently the smaller impact on the balance sheet also speaks for the assumption of liability. An amount need only be entered on the debit side if it is certain that a claim will be asserted. For cases where the assertion of claims is primarily probable, a reserve for uncertain debts must be created (§ 249 HGB). As a rule, there is only a note at the bottom of the balance sheet regarding the liability situation (§ 251 HGB).[253]

A private bank, in making organizational and financing decisions, has the freedom to conduct certain business through its own departments or to establish or acquire subsidiaries for that purpose. In so doing it must repeatedly make a decision about whether and to what extent a direct contribution of capital should be undertaken, or whether a limited or unlimited assumption of liability for the subsidiary should occur. As has been set forth above, unlimited liability can be assumed by fully liable partners of a private partnership or by means of a comfort letter or a covenant to cover losses. The freedom of choice with respect to the financial instrument thus encompasses the freedom to choose the legal form.

This is evidenced by the existence of different legal forms for private financial institutions. Through the not uncommon choice of operating private banks in the form of private partnerships[254], personal liability is instituted as a financial instrument. This is also recognized in bank supervision law through the additional amount in the liable capital requirements of 10, 10a KWG.[255]

Private banks, too, receive better financing terms by virtue of the parent company's liability, such that in comparison, there is no benefit for public companies.[256]

---

[253] The balance sheet annotation requirement pursuant to 251 HGB regarding liability circumstances does indeed have an impact on the parent company's own scope of financing.

[254] *Cf.* Section D III 3 a), aa), *supra.*

[255] *Cf.* Section B IV 2, *supra.*

[256] On the significance of group company liability and comfort letters as features of credit, *cf. Lwowski/Groeschke,* WM 1994, p. 613.

The significance of liability, as a financing instrument, for the good standing of banks is demonstrated by the rating of private banks. As to the stand-alone rating, which does not take into account the liability situation of the parent company, private banks are clearly downgraded in comparison to the traditional rating.[257] The IBCA individual rating of Commerzbank, a B/C, is significantly lower than the traditional rating. The downgrading of BHF-Bank to a C+ by the Moody's stand-alone rating, compared with a traditional A1, seems to demonstrate the significance of liability considerations. As to the stand-alone rating, only *Deutsche Bank* received the highest grade.

Despite all fundamental doubts with respect to the concept of the stand-alone rating, these ratings do indeed tend to show that the significance of liability considerations in the private credit business is no less than with respect to public banks.

Among the various financing options of private companies, the assumption of liability by a partner takes on particular significance. The support of subsidiaries without negatively affecting liquidity or the balance sheet plays an important role primarily for private banks.

2. Free choice between liability and capital, even for the state

The state has broad organizational discretion in the decision concerning the form in which its public functions are to be executed and in choosing the legal form for public enterprises.[258]

According to the private investor principle, the usual general rule applicable to private banks regarding the freedom of choice of legal form, together with the choice between liability or capital, is also applicable to the state with respect to financial institutions under public law.

The support of subsidiaries without negatively impacting liquidity or the balance sheet, whether by means of the legal form of the company, comfort letters or covenants to cover losses, all of which are possible for private companies, must also be an option for the state.

---

[257] Extensive treatment of this topic in Section E III 3 d) aa), *infra*.

[258] *Cf.* Section B III 3, *supra*.

Within the framework of this broad organizational discretion in the choice of legal form for public companies, the state also must take into consideration budgetary objectives. Discrimination against private companies regarding the free choice of legal form would impede the public authorities in their objective to preserve the liquidity of the public budget, and thus would be contrary to good business practice.

3. The absence of a consideration as an indicator for a subsidy

a) The absence of a commission on guarantee as an indicator for a subsidy

It is questionable whether the complete absence of a consideration or of a reasonable consideration for the assumption of liability as an element of enhanced debt financing recommends the acceptance of a subsidy or must be seen as an indicator for a subsidy.[259]

The customariness of a commission on guarantee is assumed in the German Foreign Tax Relations Act (AStG) in that it construes a commission on guarantee when a German company issues a surety for a foreign subsidiary.[260]

The Commission assumes that the absence of a commission on guarantee is evidence of a subsidy. In the context of the subsidy proceeding regarding *Hibeg/Krupp/Bremer Vulkan,* the federal government took the position that the securities and guarantee commissions that in principle are prescribed in the state surety directive would be unnecessary since a public company was at issue, such that the guarantee commission ultimately would only have meant a book transfer.[261] The Commission disagreed, and stated: *"Alone the fact that HIBEG was released from having to provide securities and from having to pay a commission on guarantee already constitutes a subsidy."*[262] This makes it clear that different public budgets may not be seen simply as a single unit. In principle, public companies must also pay a consideration if they come to benefit from state services. Such an obligation to pay a consideration may also arise from the assumption of a surety.

---

[259] This is the view of *Möschel,* Banken und Wettbewerb, p. 481, and *Seidel,* EG-Binnenmarkt und öffentliche Unternehmen, pp. 343, 350.

[260] *Michalski,* WM 1994, 1229, 1231.

[261] Commission dated 4-6-1993, OJ. L 185 dated 7-28-1993, pp. 44-45.

[262] *Loc. cit.,* p. 47.

Möschel comments that public banks do not distribute any profits and the responsible authority does not receive any consideration for its guarantee pledge. He points out that a reasonable investor would never pledge his assets without demanding a consideration in return.[263]

If one were to proceed on the assumption of there being a requirement for a common market consideration, the fulfillment of public functions cannot be considered to be a common market consideration within the meaning of Article 92,1 EC Treaty.[264] For only Article 90,2 EC Treaty provides for the consideration of the fulfillment of public functions.[265]

b) Uncommonness of a direct consideration for private bank liability

With respect to the consideration issue, the value the assumption of liability would have if this function had been acquired against payment on the market could be of decisive importance.

In assessing the common market behavior of the state, it does not matter whether and under what conditions a public enterprise can obtain an assumption of liability by third parties. For the behavior of a typical private investor it is a matter of decisions on the part of a current or potential shareholder, not a matter of to whom and under what conditions a bank or other commercial surety extends credits or sureties.

In order to compare guarantor liability with liability and financing structures in the private banking sector, it therefore does not matter when and under what conditions third parties would have assumed liability for a financial institution.

It can only be a matter of the consideration that an investor would have requested from the company for the assumption of unlimited liability or for the surety, as the case may be. At the same time it could be questionable whether the standard of a corporation or a partnership should be applied.

---

[263] *Cf.* the interview with *Möschel* in Handelsblatt dated 4-22-1996, pp. 33, 34; similarly *Gleske,* p. 342.

[264] But this is the view of *Scherer/Schödermeier,* ZBB 1996, pp. 165, 174, who see institutional burden and guarantor liability as an appropriate consideration for the fulfillment of public functions by savings banks and *Landesbanken;* similarly *Schneider/Busch,* EuZW 1995, pp. 602, 606. *Koenig,* EuZW 1995, pp. 595, 600, on the other hand, only finds a connection to the fulfillment of public functions with respect to institutional burden, but not for guarantor liability.

[265] On the difference between a consideration and an adjustment of a public disadvantage, *cf. von Wallenberg,* in Gedächtnisschrift f. *Grabitz,* pp. 867, 872.

If one were to start with a partner of a partnership (which seems justified given the parallelism to guarantor liability), then it is clear that the partner cannot demand a separate consideration for his unlimited liability by virtue of partnership law because of the advantages that have resulted with respect to his credit solvency. The same is true with respect to the extension of an additional security, for example a land charge for a credit to the company from a third party: the partner will hardly expect a consideration in the form of a credit security commission.

A GmbH-partner, on the other hand, is much more likely to request consideration for providing securities.

In the practice of private banks, which on the whole is relevant, no consideration is paid to the parent bank for the assumption of unlimited liability in general partnership banks.

Neither is there usually an agreement with respect to a commission or consideration for a comfort letter[266] or a covenant to cover losses.[267] The parent company considers the consideration as having been paid through future distributions.[268]

At times the legal basis for the comfort letter and covenant to cover losses is seen in the corporate relationship *(causa societatis)*, or the focus is on the continuation of the promotional activity of the supported company.[269]

The comfort letters of major German banks are not countered in the balance sheets by individually itemized returns of the subsidiaries. Neither can one find in the balance sheets of the subsidiaries any expenses associated with the aforementioned securities. This makes it clear that it is not common market practice to provide a direct consideration for the assumption of unlimited liability.

Of course one might think that the "commission on guarantee" is not explicitly set out, but it is contained in the subsidiaries' transfers of profits. Since distributions of profits, at least with respect to savings banks, are smaller than is the case for private banks[270], one could assume that there is an insufficient and inappropriate "indirect" consideration that establishes the same subsidy-like nature as guarantor liability in light of the surety effect.

---

[266] *Michalski,* WM 1994, pp. 1229, 1231.

[267] *Karsten Schmidt,* Festschrift *Werner* 1984, pp. 777ff.

[268] *Schneider/Busch,* EuZW 1995, pp. 602, 607.

[269] *Karsten Schmidt,* Festschrift *Werner,* 1984, pp. 785ff.

[270] One must keep in mind, however, that savings banks make large expenditures for the welfare of the public and thereby relieve the guarantor with respect to its obligations.

One must keep in mind, however, that private investors are not solely motivated by regular distributions of profits (dividends), but also take into consideration the increase in net asset value in the form of rising share prices.

This is also made clear in the communiqué of the Commission on public companies (text no. 35), which focuses on *"comparable private companies' customary payment of interest by means of dividend payments or increases of capital."* It is conceivable for an investor to grant an unlimited assumption of liability to a subsidiary by means of a comfort letter or a covenant to cover losses, expecting in return not a commission fee, but rather an increase in the company's intrinsic value. The current net asset value of the savings banks and *Landesbanken* exceeds the value of the original capitalization many times over; thus one can proceed on the assumption of a regular increase of the responsible authority's assets. The encumbrance of the founding body and guarantor with contingent liabilities would appear to be unlikely to offset this increase.

4. Preliminary conclusion

Assuming that there are refinancing advantages for savings banks and *Landesbanken* by virtue of their legal form, based on the private investor test one must reject the characterization of these advantages as a subsidy.

III. Proof and quantification of a benefit

Inasmuch as an economic benefit seems likely in individual cases for *Landesbanken* with respect to refinancing, the question arises as to the proof and quantification of the benefit.

1. The quantification of "standing subsidies"

The quantification of a subsidy gives rise to the problem of the comparability of low-interest credits, guarantees and one-time contributions. The Commission is trying to solve this problem by means of a complicated mathematical conversion into a contribution that is of equal value, is non-recurring, and given at the time the subsidy is approved.

For purposes of this "subsidy equivalent"[271], one must focus on the financial advantage to the company, and not on the costs incurred by the state.[272]
In the case of guarantees for raising of loans from third parties, the savings of interest compared to standard market conditions without such guarantees must be calculated. The difference in interest rates must be multiplied by the amount of the loan, or the nominal value of the loan, as the case may be, in order to determine the annual savings in interest expenses. Finally, in order to convert the standing subsidy into a one-time contribution, one must take into consideration the term of the obligation.

The fact that guarantor liability entails liability for an undetermined amount could be particularly problematic for purposes of quantification. The presence of a subsidy depends further on the behavior of the benefitting company; the conditions for a subsidy are supposed to be met only when the company has acquired lower interest capital for itself with the help of public liability. This runs somewhat counter to recognized Commission precedents that in principle the existence of a subsidy must be presumed as early as the moment of the assumption of liability, and not at a later time, *i.e.* the time when the surety is actually utilized.[273]

2. The Commission's attempt at quantification by means of a ratings comparison

In its internal deliberations the Commission has tried to quantify an improvement of the refinancing of the *Landesbanken* caused by guarantor liability. To this end the actual average financing costs of the *Landesbanken* were supposed to be compared to the hypothetical average financing costs in a case where institutional burden and guarantor liability are no longer granted.

---

[271] *Cf. Petersen,* pp. 9, 14.

[272] *Petersen,* p. 14.

[273] In a draft communiqué of the Commission on the application of Articles 92 and 93 EC Treaty to state subsidies that are granted in the form of sureties, dated March 7, 1995, text no. 1.2, it reads: "*The subsidy-like character of state sureties is often not recognized at all by the authorities who grant them, or is not recognized at the point in time when it would have to be recognized, that is, at the point in time when the sureties were granted and not at the point of time when their mobilization is required.*"

Ratings (*i.e.* indices of a company's credit solvency developed by special agencies) were used as an aid in the calculation. The actual rating of *Landesbanken* was compared with a hypothetical rating developed by the agencies that excluded guarantor liability. Average financing costs on a specified financial market were assigned to these ratings and compared with one another. In the opinion of the Commission, the financing advantage fluctuates between DM 250 million and DM 500 million[274], depending on the size of the bank.

3. Proof and quantification of a benefit by means of credit ratings

As evidence of a benefit by means of an improvement of refinancing terms it is argued that public-law banks have a better credit rating as a result of the unlimited liability of the state, and that consequently they have lower interest expenses on the international financial markets than would be the case without this liability.

Such credit ratings provided by private rating agencies are relied upon on international financial and capital markets, particularly in the United States, for purposes of assessing the standing of a debtor and hence also of assessing the risk of an investment.

a) Description of the rating system

aa) The concept of ratings

A rating can be defined as an opinion, expressed by means of a symbol, concerning the ability and legal commitment of a state or private issuer to fulfill payment obligations associated with the issuance of certain securities in a timely and complete fashion, or concerning the general credit solvency of an issuer in the sense of an estimation of the probability if its insolvency.[275] Ratings serve as a source of information for market participants and thus increase market transparency.

---

[274] *Cf.* "Konkurs unmöglich", Der Spiegel dated 4-8-1996, pp. 102, 104.

[275] Definition from *Everling,* Der langfristige Kredit 1991, p. 272.

Private rating agencies from the United States and Great Britain currently rate more than 4500 companies and corporations throughout the world.[276] Market leaders by far in international ratings are the U.S. agencies *Moody's Investors Services and Standard & Poor's.*

The rating agencies developed systems of letters and numbers to assess the credit solvency of a debtor. The various rating systems extend from A through D and encompass numerous intermediate stages designated with additional letters and numbers.[277] The triple A rating (AAA) is the highest credit solvency level and represents first-class international creditworthiness. The ratings are updated at various time intervals and among other things are published over electronic information systems.

In addition to the company-specific risk, important assessment criteria for the rating of private companies are also the issuance-specific risk, the risk of the line of business[278] and the country-related risk, *i.e.* the rating of the state in which the company has its place of business.[279] The country rating is normally the upper limit of the company rating (the "sovereign ceiling").[280] If there are comfort letters, sureties or guarantees of a parent company, this is taken into consideration in the rating of a subsidiary.[281]

bb) The rating of financial institutions under public law

In the rating undertaken by the U.S. rating agency Moody's Investors Service on 3-14-195[282], 11 banks in Germany achieved a triple A or best possible rating: in addition to two private banks, there were three *Landesbanken* and six special state financial institutions.

---

[276] *Cf. Cantor/Packer,* The Credit Rating Industry, Federal Reserve Bank of New York Quarterly Review, 19, pp. 1, 4ff., quoted from *v. Randow,* ZBB 1995, pp. 140, 141.

[277] *Moody's Investors Services* rates banks with the designations Aaa, Aa1, Aa2, Aa3, A1, A2, A3, Baa1, Baa2, Baa3, etc. *Standard & Poor's* rates debtors from A to D: AAA, AA, A, BBB, BB, B, CCC, CC, C, D.

[278] *Cf. Serfling/Pries,* Die Bank 1990, pp. 381, 382; *Ebenroth/Daum,* WM 1992, Supplement 5, pp. 1, 4.

[279] *Cf. Everling,* Der langfristige Kredit 1991, 384; *Ebenroth/Daum,* WM 1992, Supplement 5, pp. 1, 4.

[280] *Everling,* Credit Rating durch internationale Agenturen, 1991, pp. 140f.

[281] *Cf. Everling,* Die Bank 1991, pp. 608, 610.

[282] *Cf.* Handelsblatt dated 3-24-1995.

Moody's rating of August 1995 shows triple A ratings for eight German banks. In addition to Deutsche Bank, Dresdner Bank and Bayerische Vereinsbank, there were four *Landesbanken* and DSL Bank. An additional six *Landesbanken* received a rating of Aa1. The Standard & Poor's rating agency gave a triple A rating to four *Landesbanken,* and an AA rating to two *Landesbanken* in August 1995. The British rating agency IBCA also gave nine *Landesbanken* a triple A rating.[283]

In part, the rating agencies justified their good ratings of public banks specifically with guarantor liability and institutional burden.

The narrow rating range of public banks is attributed to the cohesion of the states resulting from the constitutional distribution of income and the financial equalization. The different ratings that nevertheless exist for individual banks are explained among other things by the fact that the chains of liability that exist as a result of the different forms of guarantor liability of savings bank associations and regional administrative bodies can lead to a delay of the guarantee obligation.[284] Additional reasons for the existing differences in credit solvency are the different economic and financial strengths and the independent spending and investment policies of the states.[285]

Thus without exception *Landesbanken* receive a consistently good to very good rating from the major agencies on international financial markets.[286]

---

[283] *Cf.,* among others, Handelsblatt dated 8-28-1995, p. 33.

[284] FAZ dated 3-17-1995, p. 24. For example, the state of Hessen is no longer the guarantor for HeLaBa. The savings banks are guarantors and shareholders of HeLaBa; the local authorities are accountable as guarantors for the savings banks, and the lands of Hessen and Thuringia are ultimately accountable for the local authorities if the local savings banks must assume liability for HeLaBa, *Cf.* Handelsblatt dated 8-24-1995.

[285] In Standard & Poor's Rating Report Germany, August 1995, it is stated:
"None of the ratings are based on the standing of the banks" (p. 3). "The only reason for the higher investment rating of *Landesbanken* is the economic and financial strength of the states that guarantee the banks" (p. 5).
"Changes in the rating are possible
- if the standing of a German state, upon which the bank's rating is based, improves or deteriorates,
- in the event of privatization" (p. 3).

[286] The *Landesbanken* are rated by Standard & Poor's, Moody's, IBCA, Bankwatch, Fitch, and Japan Credit Rating Agency, among others.

These ratings correspond on average to the ratings of the largest German private banks Deutsche Bank, Dresdner Bank, Commerzbank, Bayerische Vereinsbank and Bayerische Hypotheken- und Wechselbank.

cc) Test approach for a ratings comparison

For the subsidy test it does not matter whether the benefitting company is placed in a better position than other companies as the result of the measure, *i.e.* whether the *Landesbanken* perhaps enjoy better terms than private banks. Rather, the improvement of one's own situation as a result of the measure compared to what that situation would have been without the measure is decisive for determining the nature of a subsidy.[287] However, one requirement would be that guarantor liability be considered as a measure within the meaning of subsidy law, which must be rejected according to the view presented here.[288]

Thus it would be necessary to determine first whether the public banks would have lower ratings if guarantor liability and institutional burden were omitted, and second whether less favorable refinancing terms would be associated with this. The latter depends on whether the rating actually influences investment and financing decisions, and thereby the refinancing terms of public banks.

b) The impact of ratings on decisions to grant credit or to invest

aa) Quality and objectivity of the rating

By means of ratings the transparency of the market is increased and the cost of information for investors and hence also the offering expenses for the issuer are lowered. For these reasons, as a rule both investors and issuers pay for the rating. However, in Germany doubts have been raised in private banking circles[289]

---

[287] *Cf.* also *Gleske,* p. 336.

[288] *Cf.* Section D II, *supra.*

[289] One board member of a German bank is quoted as having said, "We don't know with respect to the rating agencies where the pedantry of the young academic stops and the basic attitude of a modern form of colonialism begins.", Handelsblatt dated 6-10-1994. The chief executive officer of the Federal Association of German Investment Companies *(Bundesverband deutscher Investmentgesellschaften)* is quoted as follows: "We don't need this kind of subjective rating by private agencies.", quoted in *Beier/Heuser,* Das Wertpapier 6/1995, p. 12; *cf.* other references in *v. Randow,* ZBB 1995, p. 141.

and in legal scholarship[290] as to the quality and objectivity of the ratings. The criticism is directed against the concentration of power and the associated uncontrolled interference in the business policies of issuers and against the rating agencies' lack of knowledge with respect to developed legal and economic structures in different countries. For these reasons Japanese and German companies in particular are heavily critical of the rating agencies from the United States. And not least for this reason there was an attempt – since abandoned – on the part of various European companies to establish a European rating agency.[291]

There were discussions with respect to a statutory regulation of the rating process with license requirements in order to ensure minimum qualification standards and independence.[292]

A market failure establishing the need for regulation could exist because in competition for market share, a "race to the bottom" on the part of the rating agencies could lower the standards for a triple A rating.[293] There would be the danger of "rating shopping."

On the other hand, due to the dominant market position of the two market leaders Standard & Poor's and Moody's, there are significant barriers to entry into the rating market.[294] Standard & Poor's in particularly is increasingly acquiring shares in smaller rating agencies specializing in national markets.[295]

---

[290] *Serfling/Pries,* Die Bank 1990, 381; *v. Randow,* ZBB 1995, pp. 144ff.; *v. Randow,* ZBB 1996, pp. 85ff., all with additional references.

[291] *Cf. Everling,* Die Bank 1991, p. 308.

[292] *Ebenroth/Daum,* WM 1992, Supplement 5, pp. 1, 8. *Cf.* also *v. Randow,* ZBB 1995, pp. 144ff., who does not believe regulation is necessary due to the self-healing powers of the market.

[293] *v. Randow,* ZBB 1995, p. 146, cites an example from the U.S. capital market, where in connection with a fight for market share lower standards for the assignment of a triple A rating were detected.

[294] There is talk of a "vicious circle of dependencies", because an issuer only retains an agency if it is sure that the outcome will promise improved conditions on the capital markets. This improvement of conditions, in turn, depends on the familiarity and acceptability of the agency. Thus a new agency can find virtually no companies for which its rating promises tangible benefits with respect to a securities offering. *Cf. Everling,* Die Bank 1991, pp. 308, 314.

[295] For a highly critical assessment, *Everling,* Die Bank 1991, pp. 308, 311.

One could take the view that there is a serious danger of the dependence of the rating agencies on issuers, because issuers are the source of 80% of the rating agencies' income.[296] The probability of being rated even without having requested it could exert an indirect pressure on issuers to retain rating agencies.[297] Various German companies were sharply critical of Moody's because in undertaking unrequested ratings it exerted indirect pressure on the companies to retain a rating agency.[298] In this context, the questions of the issuers' right of appeal and of possible publication bans by the issuers may also be relevant in individual cases. In order to promote their reputation, rating agencies take care to avoid any appearance of financial or structural involvement.[299] The announcement made by agencies that their fee structure is not negotiable is understood in this context.[300]

Criticism of the declaratory value of the rating is focused on the lack of transparency of the agencies' assessment formulae.[301] Another limitation of the declaratory value of the rating lies with its ordinality; there is only a categorization into groups with similar risks, which precludes the possibility of assigning concrete numbers with respect to determining interest risk factors.[302]

bb) Acceptance of the rating and its relevance to decision making

A relevant benefit exists if the actual financing costs are demonstrably improved by a better rating. In principle, this is independent of the informational content and objectivity of the rating. Rather, it depends on the actual acceptance of the rating and the influence it exerts on the investment decisions of players on the financial market. However, there is an indirect connection, via the control function of the market, between the quality of

---

[296] *Cf. v.Randow,* ZBB 1995, pp. 140, 147.

[297] *Cf. v.Randow,* ZBB 1995, pp. 140, 141.

[298] *Cf.* Süddeutsche Zeitung dated 7-27-1996, p. 27; for an extensive treatment of unrequested ratings and their assessment under competition law and antitrust law.

[299] *Cf. v.Randow,* ZBB 1995, pp. 140, 148, on the ownership structure of the large U.S. rating agencies. A detailed treatment of the ownership structure of the rating agencies also in Everling, Die Bank 1991, p. 151, 154.

[300] *v.Randow,* ZBB 1995, pp. 140, 147.

[301] *Serfling/Pries,* Die Bank 1990, pp. 381, 383; *Schroeder,* Der langfristige Kredit 1995, p. 6.

[302] *Cf. Serfling/Preis,* Die Bank 1990, pp. 381, 383.

the rating and its relevance to investor decision making. If the informational value of the rating declines perceptibly in the eyes of investors due to incorrect assessments, then at least experienced institutional investors will not make use of the rating over the longer term.

To this extent doubts as to the objectivity and declaratory value of a rating also give rise to doubts as to its relevance to decision making.

The acceptance of ratings agencies depends on trust developed over a long period of time. With every rating given, investors receive more data for comparison; the rating service is becoming continuously more valuable. Moody's and Standard & Poor's have been providing ratings since the beginning of the century. The importance of ratings for the capital market in the United States, where over 98% of industrial bonds are provided with ratings, is decisively attributable to this long tradition and corresponding experience of the rating agencies.

Under U.S. and Japanese supervisory law the ratings of certain agencies are officially recognized.[303] Certain institutional investors are prohibited from investing in securities that carry a lower rating than "BB".[304]

By contrast, in Germany the palpable increase in the influence of ratings is still considered on the whole to be relatively minor.[305]

The small influence of ratings in Germany is attributable in part to the fact that previously German companies, by international comparison, have obtained only a small portion of their financing through bonds, choosing for the most part to take out bank credits instead.

This is also attributable to the fact that until the end of 1990, the issuance of bearer bonds or bonds made out to order was subject to state approval pursuant to §§ 795, 808a BGB.[306] Proposals for the quasi statutory recognition of ratings in security-law investment regulations as constituent facts for credit solvency have not gained acceptance.[307]

---

[303] *Cf. Everling,* Die Bank 1991, pp. 151, 156.

[304] *Cf. Everling,* Die Bank 1991, pp. 151, 156; *Breuer,* WM 1991, 1109.

[305] *Cf. v. Randow,* ZBB 1995, pp. 140, 141, with additional references; *Serfling/Pries,* Die Bank 1990, pp. 381, 384; *Everling,* Die Bank 1991, pp. 308, 311.

[306] *Ebenroth/Daum,* WM 1992, Supplement 5, pp. 1, 2; *Serfling/Pries,* Die Bank 1990, pp. 381, 384; *v. Randow,* ZBB 1995, pp. 140, 141.

[307] *Cf. v. Randow,* ZBB 1995, p. 140, 156.

The fact that several public banks specifically solicit business with improved creditworthiness through guarantor liability[308] is evidence of the increased significance of credit ratings. The decision to request a rating is justified by the *Landesbanken* with the argument that many potential foreign investors are not familiar with the public banks in Germany and the underlying system of liability.[309]

One must assume that on the German market other criteria besides ratings play a more important role in investment decisions. Among them, for example, are the standing of the issuer, the stability, regularity and breadth of its market presence, and the degree to which investors are familiar with it. Of particular significance is market manipulation, i.e. the ability and willingness of the issuer to stabilize stock prices in a crisis situation. For the special case of *Landesbanken*, the aspect of economic integration with savings banks must be pointed out. The *Landesbanken* have access to extraordinary distribution possibilities over the broad savings bank branch network.

Evidence of whether and to what extent the players on the financial market in Germany support their decisions with ratings is dubious and merely based on assumptions. One must reject the notion of there being a mathematical/functional relationship whereby the rating represents the interest rate risk factor.

---

[308] Landeskreditbank Baden-Württemberg, for example, advertises as follows (p. 5): *"Landeskreditbank has the benefit of a Aaa/AAA rating for . . . its obligations. This excellent standing demonstrates not only the solid financial basis of Landeskreditbank, but is also the result:*
1. of its legal position as an institution under public law;
2. of its 100% affiliation with the state of Baden-Württemberg and the resulting direct and unlimited support of the state;
3. of the extraordinary economic and financial strength of the state;
4. of the constitutionally-based and financial policy-based relationships between Baden-Württemberg and the Federal Republic of Germany;
5. of the AAA rating of the Federal Republic of Germany."

[309] *Cf. Adam, Der langfristige Kredit 1996, pp. 38, 39; Werner Schmidt, ZfgK 1996, pp. 200, 202.*

c) Perceptible raising of capital in ratings-influenced markets?

aa) The refinancing structure of *Landesbanken*

A benefit caused by guarantor liability can only be assumed if *Landesbanken* actually seek refinancing on ratings-influenced markets.

Landesbanken and public federal banks do not have a branch network and thus have no primary access to private savings deposits.[310] Deposits and borrowings by non-banks comprised only 22.2% of business volume of *Landesbanken* in August 1995, whereas they comprised 43.8% for major banks and 43.2% across the entire banking sector.[311] The percentage of liabilities in the inter-banking sector was 34.3% for *Landesbanken*, compared with 36.5% for major banks and 25.9% across the entire banking sector. The major share of refinancing is undertaken via bearer bonds, which comprised 37.2% of business volume for *Landesbanken*. Across the entire banking sector the percentage is 21.4%, 5% for major banks, and 6% for savings banks.

Concerning the influence of ratings, it must be taken into consideration with respect to bonds that the *Landesbanken* for the most part seek refinancing through the issuance of *covered* bonds, *i.e.* through mortgage bonds and municipal bonds. The capital market statistics of the Central Bank of Germany show that on average over the last ten years, covered bonds have comprised 77.6% of all bonds in the public sector. The rating plays no significant role with respect to these securities because the satisfaction of creditors is secured *in rem* by covered stock (§ 6 Public Bond *[Pfandbriefe]* Act (ÖPG)).

Thus only the remaining naked bonds are relevant to the difficult question of the quantification the influence of ratings.

These naked bonds are mainly sold on the domestic and European capital market. Only a very small percentage of *Landesbank* refinancing – less than 5% according to information provided by one *Landesbank* (WestLB) – takes place on the strongly ratings-influenced U.S. market. On the European market the influence exerted by the rating on the investment decisions of players on the financial market is likely to be very slight.

---

[310] A detailed treatment of the refinancing of *Landesbanken* in *Adam,* Der langfristige Kredit, No. 2, 1996, pp. 38, 40.

[311] The data are taken from the Monatsbericht October 1995 of the Central Bank of Germany, statistical portion, p. 21.

For *Landesbanken*, normally less than 10% of all bonds issued in various currencies are rated.

For the question of rating influence, one must keep in mind that, as to rated bonds, not all customers are influenced by the rating in making their investment decision.

On the other hand the rating of a bond plays a role in investment decisions with respect to non-rated bonds. Thus there are both rated bonds that are not influenced by ratings, as well as non-rated bonds that are influenced by ratings. For this reason the percentage share of rated bonds is not a direct indication for the percentage of ratings-influenced investment decisions.

Based on the foregoing, one must proceed on the assumption that in any case significantly less than one-fifth of bonds issued by *Landesbanken* are influenced by ratings.

bb) The refinancing structure of savings banks

As to the question of whether savings banks as compared to private banks enjoy advantageous refinancing terms that can constitute a benefit, one must take into consideration that savings banks – unlike *Landesbanken* – normally lack direct access to international financial markets.

Savings banks are not rated by rating agencies with the exception of a few particular cases. In their financing structures they differ considerably from *Landesbanken*. Bonds make up only 6% and inter-bank loans 14% of the business volume of savings banks.[312]

Typically, savings banks carry out their refinancing by means of deposits. On average, the deposits of non-banks comprised over 68.8% of the business volume of savings banks in August 1995. Over half of these were savings deposits. Yet the average amount of the individual deposits is relatively small.

It could be questionable whether, in the area of deposits, the more favorable terms of savings banks as compared with private banks represent a benefit.

Non-institutional investors, with savings deposits of importance to savings banks, also orientate themselves by the security of the deposit and the credit solvency of the bank. It could suggest itself that savings banks, because of the guaranteed safety of the deposits by the state, can pay lower interest than would otherwise be required.

[312] *Cf.* Monatsbericht October 1995 of the Central Bank of Germany, statistical portion, p. 21.

For the question of benefit it does not matter whether in this respect the savings banks are on a better or equal footing as against their private competitors. Furthermore, this question would give rise to the problem of whether the higher volumes of deposits or the more favorable interest terms really are attributable to the public liability or rather if they are attributable to the comprehensive services offered by savings banks and to their extensive branch network.

Ultimately it is a matter of whether savings banks succeed in achieving more favorable terms for their customers or depositors as a result of the liability, and thus are in a better position than would be the case if public liability hypothetically were excluded as a factor.[313] The structural preservation mechanisms of the banking sector in the form of minimum capitalization requirements and deposit guarantees must also be taken into consideration.

It is recognized that benefits to which all companies active within a member country have access are not subsidies.[314] Non-bank savings deposits, which are of such importance to savings banks, would also be virtually completely secured at private banks by means of the Deposit Guarantee Fund of the Federal Association of German Banks (see Section B IV 3, *supra*). The private deposit guarantee system guarantees the full repayment of each individual non-bank customer deposit that does not exceed 30% of the liable capital of the bank. At the end of 1994, the secured amount per deposit averaged ca. DM 70 million. The deposits of non-bank customers of private banks thereby enjoy nearly absolute security that is only limited by the existence of the Guarantee Fund itself in the event of a serious general banking crisis.

The deposit guarantee system for private banks in Germany, which is recognized by the government and required per EU directive, guarantees approximately the same security for the greatest portion of savings deposits at almost all private and public financial institutions. The security of the deposits thus would seem to be a parameter of competition only to the extent that private investors are unaware of the security system or to the extent that higher transaction costs in connection with recourse to the Deposit Guarantee Funds are assumed.

---

313 For the question of a subsidy a comparison of the situation prior to the measure with the situation after the measure is decisive, European Court of Justice dated 7-2-1974, Rs. 173/73, Italien/Kommission, Judgement 1974, 709, 720, marginal note 17; *cf. Rawlinson* in *Lenz* Art. 92, marginal note 12.

314 *Wenig* in *v.d. Groeben/Thiesing/Ehlermann*, Art. 92, marginal note 16; *Caspari*, p. 79.

The statutory protection of deposits at savings banks by means of guarantor liability thus only creates a security that already has existed for a long time and is typical for private banks. Thus savings banks are thereby enabled to take part in competition under equal conditions.

Therefore one must not expect that savings banks receive more favorable terms in the form of lower interest rates from their depositors because of guarantor liability.

The dogmatic classification of these parallels to the private Deposit Guarantee Fund as the absence of an economic benefit, the common market behavior of a private investor[315], or as imperceptible distortion of competition[316], is ultimately of no importance.

An advantage of savings banks in competition for private deposits could be assumed to the extent that in the face of an impending systemic crisis, depositors, acting on the presumption of greater security with savings banks, transfer their assets to state-secured financial institutions.[317]

One can conclude that there is no benefit for savings banks resulting from guarantor liability. A different conclusion is only possible in the event of an extraordinarily high percentage of financing on international financial markets or in the event of a banking crisis that shakes confidence in private banking for a long time.

---

315 A classification using the private investor test would require that one understand the Deposit Guarantee Fund – contrary to its purpose as set forth in the by-laws, and to its legal form, which specifically precludes any legal claims to services from the fund – as voluntary insurance that any private bank can take out upon payment of a premium, in order to solicit business using the competitive parameter of deposit security. Since savings banks do not pay any apparent premium or consideration for the liability, guarantor liability would ultimately not be justifiable as common market behavior. In this case one would nevertheless need to take into consideration that there are institutional security systems for savings banks that function much like the Deposit Guarantee Fund with respect to deposits (*cf.* Section B IV 3).

316 *Cf.* Section H I, *infra.*

317 See Section G, *infra.*

d) Downgrading of a rating for a hypothetical discontinuation of guarantor liability: The stand-alone rating

The qualification of favorable financing terms as a subsidy depends on how the players on the financial market and the rating agencies would *subjectively* assess the credit solvency of public financial institutions if there were no guarantor liability. In this connection it does not matter whether the rating of public banks is better than that of private banks.

Recently Moody's and IBCA, among others, have introduced a so-called stand-alone rating. With the stand-alone rating the creditworthiness of private banks on the inter-bank market is supposed to be assessed without consideration of the backing of the guarantors or group parent companies.

aa) The concept of the stand-alone rating

In its Bank Financial Strength Rating (BFSR) of August 1995, the U.S. rating agency Moody's Investors Service assesses the financial strength of financial institutions without taking into consideration support mechanisms such as comfort letters, guarantees or guarantor liability. Moreover, country-related risks are also excluded.

Using a rating scale from A to E, 21 German banks are ranked. The BFSR ranking is published together with previous ratings for short-term and long-term liabilities.

According to the agency, the new rating is not calculated to assess the risks of a bank's ability to meet its payment obligations. Rather it is a matter of rating the probability and the extent of external support and the factors that negatively affect the inherent standing of the bank such as a poor country rating or a high national currency risk.[318] The indicator is supposed to reflect the financial strength of the bank as such. It is explicitly stated that the BFSR is supposed to be considered by investors merely as one isolated component of the existing rating. The British agency IBCA, which deals primarily with bank ratings, also assesses several *Landesbanken* without consideration of the liability circumstances (the so-called *IBCA individual).*

[318] *Cf.* Handelsblatt dated 8-28-1995, p. 33.

	Moody's	Moody's BFSR	IBCA	IBCA ind. rat.
	Status: August 1995		Status: Nov. 1995	
Deutsche Bank	Aaa	A	AAA	A
Dresdner Bank	Aaa	A	AA+	A/B
Bayer. Vereinsbank	Aaa	A	AA+	A/B
Commerzbank	Aa2	B+	AA–	B/C
Bayer. Hypothekenbank	Aa2	B+	AA	A/B
Berliner Handels- und Frankfurter Bank	A1	C+	AA–	A/B
Bayerische Landesbank	Aaa	C+	AAA	B
Bremer Landesbank/ Kreditanstalt Oldenburg	Aa1	C	AAA	B
DG Bank	A2	D+		
DSL Bank	Aaa	D+	–	–
Landesbank Berlin	Aa1	B	AAA	B
LB Hessen/Thüringen	Aaa	C+	AAA	B
LB Rheinland-Pfalz	Aa1	C+	AAA	B
LB Schleswig-Holstein	Aa1	C	AAA	–
L-Bank	Aaa	C+	–	–
NordLB	Aa1	C+	AAA	B
SüdwestLB	Aaa	C+	AAA	B
WestLB	Aa1	C	AAA	B

The rating levels of the rating agencies are based on the following definitions:

IBCA Individual Ratings – Definitions

Individual Rating A

A bank of impeccable financial condition, with a consistent record of above average performance.

Individual Rating B

A bank with a sound risks profile and without significant problems. The bank's performance has generally been in line with or better than that of its peers.

Individual Rating C

A bank which has an adequate risks profile but possesses one or more troublesome aspects, giving rise to the possibility of risk developing, or which has generally failed to perform in line with its peers.

Individual Rating D

A bank which is currently underperforming in some notable manner. Its financial condition is likely to be below average and its profitability poor. The bank has the capabality of recovering using its own resources, but this is likely to take some time.

Individual Rating E

A bank with very serious problems which either requires or is likely to require external support.

Moody's Bank Financial Strength Ratings

A

Banks rated A possess exceptional intrinsic financial strength. Typically, they will be major institutions with highly valuable and defensible business franchises, strong financial fundamentals, and a very attractive and stable operating environment.

B

Banks rated B possess strong intrinsic financial strength. Typically, they will be important institutions with valuable and defensible business franchises, good financial fundamentals, and an attractive and stable operating environment.

C

Banks rated C possess good intrinsic financial strength. Typically they will be institutions with valuable and defensible business franchises. These banks will demonstrate either acceptable financial fundamentals within a stable operating environment, or better than average financial fundamentals within an unstable operating environment.

D

Banks rated D possess adequate financial strength, but may be limited by one or more of the following factors: a vulnerable or developing business franchise; weak financial fundamentals; or an unstable operating environment.

E

Banks rated E possess very weak intrinsic financial strength, requiring periodic outside support or suggesting an eventual need for outside assistance. Such institutions may be limited by one or more of the following factors: a business franchise of questionable value; financial fundamentals that are seriously deficient in one or more respects; or a highly unstable operating environment.

Modifiers

Where appropriate, a "+" may be appended to ratings below the A level to favorably distinguish stronger banks within the category.

The *Landesbanken*, which under Moody's regular rating system were able to show either one of the two best ratings, with the exception of Landesbank Berlin (B), were rated C or C+ under Moody's Bank Financial Strength Rating. DG Bank and DSL-Bank achieve only a D+ with the BFSR. Under the regular rating, DG Bank was rated with an A2 and DSL-Bank with a triple A.

Among the private banks, Deutsche Bank, Dresdner Bank and Bayerische Vereinsbank receive the best rating of A also under the BFSR. Commerzbank and Bayerische Hypothekenbank are downgraded to a B+.

The Commission bases its comments on the assumption that the differences in ratings are clearly attributable to the public support, since such differences cannot be observed with respect to private banks.

This is somewhat true for Moody's. The theory must be questioned, however, if one is considering the IBCA individual rating. Under that rating all of the aforementioned *Landesbanken* are downgraded to a B from their traditional triple A rating. Private banks as well – with the exception of Deutsche Bank, which also received the best rating of A – are downgraded under the individual rating. Commerzbank in particular, with a B/C, was rated lower than all of the *Landesbanken*.

Hence under the stand-alone rating both public and private financial institutions tend to be similarly downgraded.

IBCA also undertakes a "legal rating". This rating orientates itself on whether the state or financially strong owners would support the financial institution in question in the event of crisis.[319]

---

[319] The following definitions apply with respect to IBCA's legal rating:

Legal Rating 1
A bank for which there is a clear legal guarantee on the part of a state to provide support OR a bank of such importance both internationally and domestically that, in our opinion, support from a state would be forthcoming, if necessary. The state in question must clearly be prepared and able to support its principal banks.

Legal Rating 2
A bank for which, in our opinion, state support would be forthcoming, even in the absence of a legal guarantee. This could be, for example, because of the bank's importance to the economy or its historic relationship with the authorities.

Legal Rating 3
A bank which has institutional owners of sufficient reputation and possessing such resources that, in our opinion, shareholder support would be forthcoming, if necessary.

Legal Rating 4
A bank for which support is likely but not certain.

Legal Rating 5
A bank which cannot rely on outside assistance.

The best rating is not assigned only when there is a state guarantee or any other type of state liability, but also if state support in the event of a crisis seems likely due to the size and significance of the bank ("too big to fail"). Hence not only a *de jure* guarantee of existence, but also a *de facto* economic guarantee of existence is taken into consideration.

All major private commercial German banks are rated with at least a 2, *i.e.* a guarantee of existence is assumed. Deutsche Bank and Dresdner Bank are even rated with 1.

In conclusion, not only public banks, but also private commercial banks are clearly downgraded by the stand-alone rating. For private banks this is true not only when the liability of the parent company is hypothetically disregarded; even when one hypothetically disregards de facto state liability in the event of crisis due to the size and importance of the afflicted bank, private banks are downgraded. To this extent it is doubtful whether public banks receive a palpable benefit from the liability of the state as compared to private banks of a certain minimum size, even if the legally protected liability for savings banks and *Landesbanken* has a different quality than an expected economic, de facto, "ad hoc" liability for private banks.

bb) Fitness of the stand-alone rating concept

The comparability of the rating with and without consideration of public liability is made more difficult due to the different scale used for the stand-alone rating. For the BFSR, Moody's uses a scale from A "extraordinary" to E "very weak", with significantly fewer graduations than the traditional rating scale. The divergent characteristics of the stand-alone rating could be suggestive of a different rating scale with different criteria. In any case no standard of comparison has been provided for the two different rating scales by the rating agencies. Therefore it would be utterly arbitrary if the BFSR scale were to be converted into the traditional rating scale by a third party, *i.e.* the Commission.

The use of identical rating scales or at least the provision of a conversion standard would be required in order to compare the rating grades.

The points of criticism cited with respect to the traditional rating are applicable to the stand-alone rating to an even greater extent. The dangers and weak points of the traditional ratings are mitigated by the control function of the market. Institutional investors can exert a disciplining function on rating agencies by threatening to turn elsewhere and hence can ensure the quality of the rating. The character of the rating as long-term investment applies here.

The stand-alone rating, on the other hand, is not subject to market control. It does not enjoy acceptance developed over time. A perceptible level of trust in a rating on the part of market participants cannot develop overnight.

The unclearness of the practical function of the BFSR is illustrated by newspaper reports, according to which Moody's was not able to respond to a request from the Association of Public Banks to make any argument at all that there was an informational need with respect to public banks for this additional rating procedure.[320] In this connection there were also rumors of pressure being applied by American underwriters, which feel at a disadvantage in light of the triple A rating for German banks.[321]

The stand-alone rating stands in blatant contradiction to the very nature of a rating. It is in keeping with the content of a rating that the coverage of securities must not be construed as an alternative to the rated standing, but rather are an integral component of the rating.[322]

The meager declaratory value of the stand-alone rating is also evident from the clearly different ratings of the two agencies, which documents the subjectivity of the rating. For example, Berliner Handels- und Frankfurter Bank (BHF-Bank), with its "A/B" rating from IBCA, received a better individual rating than all *Landesbanken*, whereas the bank was downgraded to a C+ with Moody's BFSR rating, which corresponds to the average for *Landesbanken*. Even greater differences can be seen in the ratings for Commerzbank. IBCA gave Commerzbank a lower individual rating than all *Landesbanken*, whereas Moody's BFSR rated the bank higher than all *Landesbanken*.

The stand-alone rating is based on the hypothetical exclusion of external support mechanisms and thus is a purely subjective estimation. How the market would react if guarantor liability were indeed discontinued is a matter of complete speculation.

The quantification of a benefit with the assistance of the stand-alone rating would thus encounter virtually insurmountable obstacles.

---

[320] *Cf.* Handelsblatt dated 8-28-1995, p. 33; Der langfristige Kredit 1995, p. 604.
[321] *Cf.* Handelsblatt dated 8-24-1995.
[322] *Cf. Serfling/Pries,* Die Bank 1990, p. 381.

e) An assessment of the calculation made by the Commission

The Commission has tried to quantify the improvement of refinancing terms brought about by guarantor liability by comparing the alleged average financing costs of a traditional aa1 rating for *Landesbanken* with the financing costs of a stand-alone C rating for *Landesbanken*. In the opinion of the Commission, the financing advantage ranges from DM 250 million to DM 500 million, depending on the size of the bank.[323]

This figure was derived by comparing the average remunerations paid on the U.S. capital market by respective debtors with a certain rating. On the U.S. capital market a triple A debtor pays an average of 8.09%, whereas on average A1 customers must expend 8.39% and Baa customers 8.75%. The difference between the U.S. average interest rate for the traditional rating and the U.S. average interest rate for the stand-alone rating of *Landesbanken* is then multiplied by the nominal value of *Landesbank* bonds currently in circulation.

This calculation is questionable on many fronts.

First, it is doubtful whether data relating to the U.S. capital market can be used to calculate the refinancing costs of German *Landesbanken*. *Landesbanken* acquire only a very small portion of their refinancing from the U.S. capital market.

Further, in determining the average interest rates on the U.S. capital market, data was used from numerous different economic areas, not just from financial institutions. The special features of the rating of financial institutions were not taken into consideration.

Not only is there a failure to differentiate with respect to issuers, but also with respect to the rated bonds. A meaningful calculation would at least require a differentiation according to the maturity date and remaining time until maturity of the securities.

It is also unclear why and according to what criteria Moody's data in particular were chosen for the calculation; a calculation based on the data of IBCA, which had instituted a stand-alone rating before Moody's, could conceivably have produced other results.

In addition, the standard for converting the various rating grades of the stand-alone rating into the traditional rating scale remains unclear; such a standard at least has not been purported by the rating agency.

---

[323] *Cf.* "Konkurs unmöglich", Der Spiegel dated 4-8-1996, pp. 102, 104.

The fact that private banks also typically receive support through the assumption of liability of the parent company and are also downgraded by the stand-alone rating is not taken into consideration in the Commission's attempted quantification.

To the extent that the stand-alone rating can serve at all as a standard for quantifying a benefit despite the lack of objectivity and acceptance, at the very least the following steps would need to be considered for purposes of a model calculation:

- First, the bonds that are to be compared must be differentiated according to the currencies and the markets in which they are issued, *i.e.* the U.S. market or European markets. Quite different ratings are possible for a company or *Landesbank* on the U.S. market and European markets if one starts with different agencies and classes of addressees.
- For the comparison, bonds with similar due dates or similar remaining terms must be used. Only financial institution data should be considered.
- Next, one would have to select a rating agency and/or a key designed for weighing the average of several ratings.
- To this end the stand-alone ratings must be converted into a scale that corresponds to the traditional rating.
- The average interest rates that are paid on the respective capital markets must be calculated for each level on the traditional rating scale.
- The interest rate *differences* that result from the comparison of the average interest rate for the stand-alone rating with the average interest rate for the traditional rating must be determined for each separate rating agency. From this, an average (weighted, if necessary) is calculated.
- This "stand-alone interest difference" of public banks would then need to be reduced by the amount of the "stand-alone interest difference" for private banks. This is because to the extent that the de facto liability of the state causes the stand-alone rating for private banks to be lower than their traditional rating, this must also be taken into consideration for public banks. For public banks, one may only "exclude" the legal guarantee of existence; the de facto guarantee of existence by the state, to the extent it is bestowed upon private banks, must also be conceded to public banks with respect to the benefit question. The positive elements of the consideration of the country-related risk for German private banks would, under certain conditions, also need to be considered with respect to German public banks.

- To the extent that the stand-alone interest difference of private banks is based on the liability of the parent company, this must be viewed as common market support of a subsidiary. The common market behavior of a private investor must also be conceded to the state with respect to public enterprises. A deduction for this in the form of an interest difference would need to be made.

It could be questionable to what extent the common market support – expressed in interest differences – of subsidiaries through guarantees or sureties is reduced by commission payments to the parent company. Furthermore, it must be examined whether it can be considered common for the market if every parent company contributes its credit solvency separately, or whether to this extent focus should be given to average values.

- Only this resulting "modified stand-alone interest difference" would then be multiplied by the nominal value of the relevant unsecured *Landesbank* bonds. The average amount of bonds floated by *Landesbanken* would need to be reduced by the amount of covered bonds.

f) Savings of interest expenses or of a commission on guarantee as a benefit?

To the extent that for private banks payment of a commission on guarantee for the parent company's assumption of liability is considered to be common market behavior, the question poses itself whether for purposes of quantifying the benefit the focus should be placed on the interest costs that are saved or the commission on guarantee that is saved.

In principle, the improvement of interest costs or the lower commission on guarantee could be placed on the side of the benefitting company. The lost commission on guarantee or the reduced commitment of contingency funds on the side of the subsidy grantor cannot be applied because as a rule one must proceed on the basis of the "receiver's horizon".

It is unlikely that the saved interest difference will correspond exactly to the requested commission on guarantee. It is the very nature of a surety used to *improve* financing (not: to make financing possible) that the savings in interest costs are greater than the commission on guarantee that is to be paid. For example, if a private company pays a 1% commission for a bank surety and as a result of that surety is able to obtain a reduction of the loan interest rate by 1.5%, the result would be a "common market financing advantage by surety" of 0.5%. In principle the same financing option for private banks is also available to public companies. If the state grants public companies sureties in order to improve their refinancing, then the resulting difference between the interest saved and the commission on guarantee cannot be considered a subsidy to the extent that it represents a "common market financing advantage by surety". Hence the interest savings cannot simply be seen as a benefit.

Neither does a benefit follow from the interest savings minus the commission on guarantee actually paid, as the Commission has determined.[324]

Rather, the "common market financing advantage by surety" would still need to be deducted from the difference between the interest savings and the actual commission on guarantee. In practice, the quantification of such a value would likely not be without problems. The calculation is made more difficult by the appropriate commission on guarantee that is to be charged. In the event of an inappropriate or altogether missing commission on guarantee, a hypothetical, common market commission on guarantee must be assigned. The question that raises itself here with respect to whether the commission on guarantee demanded by an affiliated company or by a third party should be assigned has already been explored above in the discussion of the private investor test.[325]

IV. Conclusions

Guarantor liability and institutional burden, as liability by virtue of organization, are not subject to subsidy control. Thus for subsidy control as behavior control, the good standing of the guarantor is fundamentally irrelevant.

Since savings banks are hardly active on international financial markets, are only rarely rated by the rating agencies and normally do not enjoy any advantages in procuring non-bank deposits due to guarantor liability, then one must reject the argument that there is a benefit in the form of improved financing due to guarantor liability.

---

[324]According to the communiqué of the Commission on public companies, text no. 38, the Commission sees the element of a subsidy associated with a guarantee in the *"difference between the interest rate that would be paid by the debtor on the free market and the interest rate actually paid as a result of the surety, minus any commissions paid for the sureties."*

[325]*Cf.* Section E II 3 b).

Whether guarantor liability constitutes an economic benefit for a *Landesbank* through an improvement of the refinancing terms is a question of an isolated case. There is no benefit for a large portion of the refinancing of *Landesbanken* by means of *covered* bonds. For naked bonds a benefit is hardly quantifiable. The stand-alone rating used for purposes of quantification is based on the hypothetical exclusion of liability mechanisms and thus is a purely subjective assessment. Contrary to the traditional rating, it does not enjoy increasing long-term acceptance and cannot be subject to any market control. Both the criteria of the stand-alone rating itself as well as its comparability with the standards of the traditional rating are unclear. To the extent that a quantification is possible at all, it would have to take into consideration the ratings of several agencies. And only the average ratings of financial institutions within the actual geographic markets concerned should be considered. The calculation would have to take into consideration, as a deduction, the statutory liability of the parent company and the de facto liability of the state.

To the extent that an economic benefit resulting from the liability of the state is assumed, this liability must be viewed as the common market behavior of a private investor. When private investors themselves have good standing, they frequently prefer an assumption of personal liability to a direct contribution of capital. The choice that is possible for private companies between the assumption of liability and a capital contribution, including the option to support subsidiaries with no or only slight encumbrances on their liquidity or balance sheet, is also open to the state.

Private companies also usually dispense with a direct consideration in return for the assumption of liability for subsidiaries. The absence of a commission on guarantee thus cannot constitute a characteristic of a subsidy.

If one were to assume the presence of a subsidy based on improved refinancing terms, then particular sanction problems would arise. The permissibility of guarantor liability would then be dependent upon the current credit solvency of the state providing the guarantee. Liability on the part of the state is not peculiar to the German banking system, but rather is common throughout the European Union. Many public banks, but also public companies from other industries, have a home country with poor credit solvency or a poor rating on international financial markets. It is possible that as a result there would be no economic benefit. However, it seems hardly proper to permit guarantor liability in some member countries but to forbid it in others. For then the prohibition would have to be constantly reviewed and adjusted, perhaps dependent on the ratings, in terms of the credit solvency of each respective country.

F. Actual contributions of capital as a subsidy?

I. Differentiation between the existence of and the execution of institutional burden

The existence of institutional burden and guarantor liability and the consequence of improved credit terms discussed above must be strictly differentiated from measures undertaken by the state in the execution of institutional burden in a crisis situation involving a public financial institution.

The latter primarily entails an actual contribution of capital to savings banks or *Landesbanken* that are experienceing financial difficulties.

The actual contribution of capital in the absence of such an emergency situation, such as was done for example in the transferal to WestLB of the Institution for Housing Promotion *(Wohnungsbauförderungsanstalt)* of the state of North Rhine-Westphalia, is not the subject of this study.

In a crisis situation it is decisive for the applicability of Article 92,1 EC Treaty whether the continuation of banking operations is made possible although a private investor would have limited his financial risk by sale, liquidation or reorganization.

II. Actual contribution of capital in a crisis situation

An actual contribution of capital represents an economic benefit that is also quantifiable. However to the extent that the transfer of financial resources is in line with the behavior of a private investor, this does not constitute a prohibited subsidy. The communiqué of the Commission on public companies, text no. 35, reads as follows on this issue:

"A contribution of capital is classified as a subsidy if it takes place under circumstances that an investor would not consent to under free enterprise conditions. As a rule this characterizes a situation in which the condition and future prospects of a company would not lead one to expect in the foreseeable future a payment of interest (by means of dividend distributions or capital increases) that would be standard for a comparable private company."

The subsidy regulations do not absolutely prevent member countries from supporting public companies during a transitional period of economic weakness. The support becomes a prohibited subsidy if over the long term the owner of the liable capital has no prospect of receiving a return on his investment.[326]

The fact that institutional burden as a capitalization obligation for a public-law financial institution is established by statutory law does not preclude the application of the subsidy prohibition. The communiqué of the Commission on public companies, text no. 36, reads as follows on this issue:

"In several member countries the investors are obligated by law to supply additional financial resources to enterprises whose capital, as the result of sustained losses, has dwindled to a certain level. . .. However, this is rather a question of a putative 'obligation', since an investor acting commercially in this type of situation would have to consider the possibility of liquidation or reduction of his investment. If it is a question of the financially more reasonable route, which nevertheless is not taken, then all contributions of capital and other state interventions thereafter would be classified as subsidies."

The subsidy prohibition under EU law, with its principle of the market-oriented investor, takes precedence over the laws establishing institutional liability in member countries and their federal provinces. Article 92,1 EC Treaty is applicable independent of the legal form of the granted benefit.[327]

For a case where a savings bank finds itself in an actual crisis situation with no prospects for future profitability, the savings bank laws provide that the responsible authority has the opportunity to dissolve and liquidate the institution. The responsible authority will only intervene with financial assistance if it is possible to duly fulfill its statutory functions. The fulfilment of functions is closely linked with profitability aspects.[328] In this respect the contribution of capital normally occurs in keeping with the principles of a market-oriented investor.

---

[326] *Cf.*, among others, European Court of Justice dated 1-14-1991, "Boussac", Judgement 1990, I-307, 361; European Court of Justice dated 3-21-1991, "Alfa Romeo", Rs. 305/89, Judgement 1991, I-1603, 1640. There are many additional references in the communiqué of the Commission on public companies, text nos. 4-23.

[327] *Cf. Wenig* in *v.d.Groeben/Thiesing/Ehlermann,* Art. 92, marginal note 6.

[328] *Cf.* Section B II 1 b), *supra.*

If the responsible authority decides to make a contribution of capital to a savings bank that does not have long-term profitability prospects, *i.e.* outside of the legal framework of institutional burden, then this constitutes a subsidy within the meaning of Article 92,1 EC Treaty.

Under certain circumstances a contribution of capital can be in keeping with the behavior of a market-oriented investor even without concrete profitability prospects for the bank or for purposes of preparing its removal from the market. The Court stated as follows in its "ENI/Lanerossi" decision:[329]

"... a private shareholder [can] reasonably contribute to a company the capital that is required to ensure its continued existence if that company is encountering temporary financial difficulties but can once again become profitable – if necessary following a reorganization.

A parent company can thus also assume the losses of one of its subsidiaries for a limited period of time in order to allow the subsidiary to cease operations under the most favorable terms possible. Such decisions cannot be based solely on the probability of an indirect material profit, but rather on other considerations, for example an effort to cultivate the image of the group or to reorient its business operations."

Under subsidy law, the limits for a permissible transfer of capital in crisis situations are thus relatively broad. The Commission too has specifically recognized that a public group holding company, just as a private company, must have the right, when withdrawing from areas of business, to *"determine the time and scope of the cessation of these activities with due regard for the consequences for the reputation and organization of the group."*[330]

The aforementioned aspect of the cultivation of the group's image may well be of particular significance for private banks. In order that the long-term objective of the group's creditworthiness is not endangered by the bankruptcy of one member of the group, the holding company will often be prepared to go beyond the requirements mandated by corporate statute or its contractual liability through comfort letters and will support the distressed subsidiary by means of voluntary payments or guarantees.[331]

---

[329] European Court of Justice dated 3-21-1991, Rs. 303/88, Italy/Commission, *"ENI/Lanerossi"*, Judgement 1991, I-1433, 1476.

[330] Communiqué, Abl. 1991 C 273/02, p. 10; *cf. Soukup,* ZögU 1995, pp. 16, 36.

[331] *Cf. Soukup,* ZögU 1995, pp. 16, 34.

The reasons set forth above for a capital contribution without profitability prospects must also be considered with respect to financial institutions under public law.

A contribution of capital from the savings bank support fund or from the guarantor to a savings bank that is unprofitable over the long term could on the whole have positive effects on the savings bank association. The concrete demand on the guarantor in the context of guarantor liability could shake faith in the continued existence of a large number of savings banks with such a lasting effect that members of the association will be willing, even in the absence of any reasonable, direct profitability prospect, to contribute capital to the savings bank that is experiencing a crisis. Yet one must still pay attention to the fact that under subsidy law the state is not obligated to contribute unlimited resources and can see to the cessation of business operations.[332]

III. Continuance of institutional burden in a crisis situation

Just as is the case for a direct contribution of capital, the continuance of liability for a company in a crisis situation may represent support that cannot be considered common market behavior, and thus constitutes a subsidy.

In the EFIM decision, the Commission considered a guarantee of the Italian government for all obligations of a company. This guarantee was based on Article 2362 of the Italian civil code, which provides for the unlimited liability for all liabilities of a wholly-owned subsidiary.

"The provision of a surety for all of a company's debts is an act that a market-oriented investor would not normally undertake without satisfying himself that the additional risk was offset by additional profits . . ..

A market-oriented shareholder would limit this "unlimited" liability by liquidating the company as soon as he has reason to fear that his debts exceed the value of his assets and that he cannot merely assume a temporary decrease in value."[333]

---

[332] *Cf.* Section B II 1 b), *supra.*

[333] Communiqué of the Commission pursuant to Article 93,2 EU Treaty to the remaining member countries and other interested parties concerning a subsidization plan of Italy for the benefit of EFIM, OJ. C 349/2 dated 12-29-1993, p. 4.

The Commission ruled that the provision of a surety and assumption of the debts of the state holding company EFIM and its 100% subsidiary must be considered to be a subsidy. The Commission found that in the future, Article 2362 is only applicable to public companies in cases comparable to those that could be assumed of a market-oriented investor.

In the exact words of the Commission:

"Upon expiration of the term prescribed in the Agreement, Article 2362 will only be applicable to public companies in cases comparable to those that could be assumed of a market-oriented investor. As of this point in time all creditors will be able to judge and rate the creditworthiness of public companies only with reference to the company's goodwill." [334]

Hence in the future the liability of the Italian government is only supposed to be effective if there are prospects for the profitability of the public enterprise.

If one applies these principles to savings banks and *Landesbanken*, attention must first be drawn to the normally healthy financial condition of savings banks and *Landesbanken*. Even in the event of past losses, in general these institutions continue to have good prospects for the adequate payment of interest. If a savings bank or Landesbank finds itself in a crisis situation without any prospects for profitability in the future, then reference must be made to the responsible authority's opportunity, provided for by law, to dissolve and liquidate the institution, or to initiate a merger.[335] If the responsible authority opts for continued existence in this situation, then according to the criteria of the EFIM decision guarantor liability represents a subsidy within the meaning of Article 92,1 EC Treaty. In such a case the assumption of a surety in the form of guarantor liability would only have legal effect with respect to liabilities that had been established in the past.

As in the case of a capital contribution, the question as to the point in time after which state liability violates Article 92,1 EC Treaty and thus becomes ineffective can only be answered on a case-by-case basis.

---

[334] EFIM decision, *loc. cit.*, p. 6.

[335] *Cf.* Section B II 1 b).

G. Special features of the banking sector: Compatibility of subsidization "to relieve a major economic disturbance" (ART. 92,3 (C))

I. Major economic disturbance

Pursuant to Article 92,3 (c) EC Treaty, subsidies may be considered to be consistent with the Common Market if they are used to relieve a major economic disturbance in a member country.

Major economic disturbances in a member country are defined as those that affect either the entire economy or at least several regions or economic sectors.[336] Related legal precedents have addressed primarily investment subsidies to create jobs.[337]

Because of its character as an exemption provision, the measures it covers must be limited in terms of time. They may not lead to a situation where the benefitting companies continue to exist at the expense of their competitors in other member countries without their having to implement structural adjustment measures.[338]

If one were to view the existence of guarantor liability as a subsidy, then its permanent approval under Article 92,3 (c) EC Treaty would be out of the question.

---

[336] General opinion, *cf. Wenig* in v.d. Groeben/Thiesing/Ehlermann, Art. 92, marginal note 60; *v. Wallenberg* in Grabitz/Hilf Art. 92, marginal note 51.

[337] *Cf. Wenig* in v.d. Groeben/Thiesing/Ehlermann, Art. 92, marginal note 62.

[338] *Wenig* in v.d. Groeben/Thiesing/Ehlermann, Art. 92, marginal note 62.

II. Special features of the banking sector

1. Measures of the state in the event of a general bank crisis

The Commission, in its 24th Competition Report of 1994, addressed the question of the extent to which the special features of the banking sector are considered in the context of the exemption provisions of Article 92 EC Treaty. According to the Report, state measures undertaken in order to prevent systemic crises, to restore the public's faith in the stability of the banking sector and to protect the smooth operation of the payment system are held to be consistent with the Common Market pursuant to Article 92,3 EC Treaty.

"State interventions are justified if all banks or large portions of the banking sector are confronted with difficulties that give rise to fears of a systemic crisis. Problems experienced by one bank or only a few banks will not necessary have as a consequence a crisis of trust in the entire system. The state should permit these banks to reorganize, liquidate (as long as a certain level of protection is ensured for small depositors) or be acquired by other financial institutions. The authorities should distinguish between illiquid and insolvent banks and only support the former with measures that help them overcome the crisis." [339]

In the decision instituting a subsidy proceeding in the case of the French bank *Crédit Lyonnais*, the Commission expressly recognized the special features of the banking sector and the high sensitivity of the financial markets:

"For the case that a crisis of trust is triggered by factors outside of banks' control, the state may feel prompted to support banks in order to avoid the negative consequences of such a systemic crisis." [340]

The Commission considered the financial measures for the benefit of *Crédit Lyonnais* to be a subsidy pursuant to Article 92,1 EC Treaty.[341]

[339] XXIV. Wettbewerbsbericht der Kommission, 1994, text no. 378.

[340] Communiqué of the Commission pursuant to Article 93,2 EU Treaty to the remaining member countries and other interested parties concerning subsidies that France has decided to grant the bank Crédit Lyonnais, Rs. C 26/95, Abl. C 121/4 dated 5-17-1995, p. 6, no. 4.

[341] Communiqué concerning Crédit Lyonnais, *loc. cit.*, p. 7, no. 4.

Next the Commission examined whether a subsidy to relieve a major economic disturbance in a member country (Art. 92,3 (c) EC Treaty) can be considered to be consistent with the Common Market. To that end the existence of a properly published, thorough and realistic plan of reorganization was verified. Accordingly, and consistent with Commission precedents with respect to rescue and reorganization subsidies[342], the requirements for the compatibility of subsidies are 1) that the measure is necessary, 2) that the future viability of the benefitting company is secured, and 3) that competition is distorted as little as possible, while protecting the public interest. In applying these three general principles to banks, the Commission takes the position that potential extreme negative effects on the financial system and the public's trust in the banking industry must be taken into consideration.[343]

2. Measures of the state for the benefit of a single financial institution

The extent to which the overall economic significance of a bank the size of *Crédit Lyonnais* can also be assumed with respect to a *Landesbank* or savings bank in crisis can only be answered on a case-by-case basis.[344]

There are no clear criteria that can be used to answer the question as to how large a bank must be in order that it may be granted a de facto guarantee of existence by the individual member countries and under what conditions the Commission considers this to be a relief of a major economic disturbance within the meaning of Article 92,3 (c) EC Treaty. Moreover, an established legal basis for this issue would imply discrimination against smaller banks. Another question that potentially could arise concerning the relationship of EU subsidy supervision to member country supervision of the credit system also apparently remains unsettled.

---

[342] Communiqué concerning Crédit Lyonnais, *loc. cit.*, p. 11, no. 7.

[343] Communiqué concerning Crédit Lyonnais, *loc. cit.*, p. 7, no. 4.

[344] *Cf. Gleske*, p. 347, who proceeds on the assumption of a general possibility of an exemption for a subsidy even with respect to difficulties experienced by a single company.

It is important for the question of the permissibility under subsidy law of state financial support for individual banks that the focus of the Commission's examination in its *Crédit Lyonnais* and *Banesto*[345] decisions was on the principle of the market-oriented investor.

Specifically, the Commission found in its 24th Report on Competition that state subsidies for the benefit of banks experiencing financial difficulties that will not necessarily have an effect on the overall banking system can also be considered consistent with the Common Market. The Commission announced its intention to establish guidelines for the application of subsidy regulations in such instances.[346]

Thus the question remains open concerning for which banks an adverse position should be considered as a general banking crisis, and when it should be considered as an individual case that does not justify any measures pursuant to Article 92,3 (c) EC Treaty.

Another case where this issue is applicable might be the rescue operation initiated in late March 1996 by the Italian government for the seventh largest Italian financial institution, Banco di Napoli, whereby the financial institution was granted the equivalent of DM 1.9 billion directly from the state.[347] The Commission has begun an investigation within the framework of its subsidy supervisory authority.

3. Incompatibility of subsidies for purposes of preventing an disturbance

Article 92,3 (c) EC Treaty merely permits the *relief* but not the *prevention* of an economic disturbance.

This is relevant to measures for the benefit of one or more financial institutions in the event of a general banking crisis.

As long as there is no concrete general banking crisis constituting a major economic disturbance, a contribution of capital to a financial institution cannot be covered by this legal exception.

---

[345] The rescue operation for the Spanish bank Banesto by the Deposit Guarantee Fund in 1994 was consistent in the eyes of the Commission with the principle of the market-oriented private investor, *cf.* XXIV. Wettbewerbsbericht der Kommission, 1994, text no. 378.

[346] *Cf.* XXIV. Wettbewerbsbericht der Kommission, 1994, text no. 378.

[347] *Cf.* Handelsblatt dated 3-28-1996, p. 25.

Even institutional burden and guarantor liability, to the extent one were to accept their quality as subsidies, could not therefore be declared consistent with the Common Market on the grounds of preventing a potential economic disturbance.

H. Distortion of competition and impairment of international trade

To the extent that on an individual case basis an actual contribution of capital or – contrary to the view taken here – institutional burden and guarantor liability were to be understood as benefits relevant to subsidy law, it would then be necessary to examine, as another prerequisite, the requirement of distortion of competition as well as the impairment of international trade.

The constituent facts of distortion of competition and impairment of international trade are important features of the subsidy prohibition under EU law. The result of the distortion of competition caused by a subsidy implies the understanding of the domestic market within which the principle of undistorted competition is valid (Article 3 (g) EC Treaty). This means that the distortion of competition is not only present when it has the direct cross-border effect of impairing competition. Even if the competition relations within a member country are affected by subsidies, this constitutes a distortion of competition within the meaning of Article 92,1 EC Treaty.

The dimension relevant to EU law is directly addressed by the requirement of the impairment of international trade. This is an issue of the delineation of EU law from domestic law. This constituent fact thus has significance as an issue of conflicting jurisdictions. Thus these two characteristics must be considered separately. The distortion of competition, even if it only affects the competition relations within a single member country, must affect trade relations within the European Union.

I. Distortion of competition

A subsidy within the meaning of Article 92,1 EC Treaty must distort or threaten to distort competition.

The issue of whether a certain intensity in the sense of perceptibility is a requirement for distortion of competition is not undisputed. In literature on this subject it is claimed that stricter standards must be applied to state measures than to private behavior. Thus, it is argued, every distortion of competition is relevant if it emanates from the state.[348] However, one must pay attention to the fact that even a threatened distortion of competition has the quality of a constituent fact, so that in the absence of a perceptibility requirement, the scope of applicability would be unnecessarily broad.[349] There are *de minimis* provisions even within the framework of the EU for subsidies for small and medium-size companies.[350] This is supposed to promote the perceptibility of actual or threatened distortions of competition.

In the opinion of the Commission and portions of the literature, every subsidy provides companies or industries advantages over competitors and thus naturally distorts competition.[351] The Court did not concur. Therefore the Commission must perform a market analysis each time demonstrating whether and to what extent competition has actually been impaired by a given measure.[352] But with respect to the scope of these demonstrations concerning distortion of competition, the demands are less stringent that within the context of Article 85, 86 EC Treaty.[353]

A market analysis in the context of subsidy supervision is frequently associated with insurmountable difficulties, however. If a widely diversified company in the procurement or financial sector receives a subsidy, it is hardly possible to determine exactly where the financial resources were used. This is particularly true for holding companies. In the case of sales of local real property to companies at below market prices, too, it is a question

---

[348] *Caspari,* p. 80; *Lefèvre,* p. 125; *Rengeling,* p. 31; *v.Wallenberg* in Grabitz/Hilf Art. 92 EC Treaty, marginal note 27; *Müller-Graff,* ZHR 1988, pp. 403, 432, differentiates between single subsidies already granted and a newly imposed subsidy system.

[349] Arguing along these lines *Wenig* in v.d.Groeben/Thiesing/Ehlermann, Art. 92, marginal note 21.

[350] Gemeinschaftsrahmen für Beihilfen zugunsten von kleinen und mittleren Unternehmen, OJ. C 213/1992, p. 2.

[351] Statement of the Commission in European Court of Justice dated 2-24-1987, Falck/Commission, Rs. 304/85, Judgement 1987, 871; *cf.* XI. Wettbewerbsbericht, 1981, marginal note 176; Advocate General *Capotari* in Philip Morris/ Commission, Rs. 730/79, Judgement 1980, 2671, 1698.

[352] European Court of Justice dated 3-13-1985, Leeuwarder Papierwarenfabrieck/ Commission, Rs.296 and 318/82, Judgement1985, 809, 822ff.; *cf. Wenig* in v.d. Groeben/Thiesing/Ehlermann, Art. 92, marginal note 20.

[353] European Court of Justice dated 9-17-1980, "Philip Morris", Rs.730/79, Judgement 1980, 2671, 2688; Rawlinson in Lenz Art. 92, marginal note 10.

as to which competition was distorted on which market.[354] The opinion expressed by the Commission that the distortion of competition lies generally in the loss-generating divisions that receive payments from the parent company[355] does not produce convincing results in every case.

It cannot matter whether aid occurs in the form of marketing assistance (in an area close to the market) or as support of basic research (in an area far from the market).[356] It is always unclear on which markets the cost relief will have a direct or indirect effect. The distortion of competition thus is regularly derivable from the cost relief that artificially strengthens the company's position on the market.

To the extent that for a *Landesbank* a benefit with respect to refinancing terms on the international financial markets would be proven, there is also a distortion of competition resulting from the corresponding cost relief[357], as far as one can assume perceptibility in the individual case.[358]

For savings banks no perceptible distortion of competition could be assumed with respect to the deposits of private customers, which are savings banks' primary business, as a result of guarantor liability.[359] The other financial institution groups in Germany, and, as a result of harmonized deposit guarantee systems, the financial institutions in neighboring member countries as well have access to similar instruments of institutional and/or deposit guarantee. Thus the deposit guarantee afforded by guarantor liability would appear unlikely to have a perceptible influence on the decision of a private investor in favor of savings banks.

---

[354] *Cf.* the comments of Petersen, p. 19.

[355] *Cf. Petersen, loc. cit.,* p. 18.

[356] *Wenig* in v.d.Groeben/Thiesing/Ehlermann, Art. 92, marginal note 20.

[357] *Cf. Koenig* EuZW 1995, pp. 595, 601.

[358] *Koenig* EuZW 1995, pp. 595, 601, proceeds on the assumption that the Commission would have to determine, in substantiated form, the financial institutions' shares on the relevant markets.

[359] *Koenig* EuZW 1995, pp. 595, 601, also assumes that with respect to the promotion mandate of savings banks there is as a rule no competitive relationship with banks from other member countries.

Maintaining the possibility of continuing business by providing an actual contribution of capital to a *Landesbank* or savings bank or through the continuation of liability in a crisis must normally be considered a distortion of competition.

The question concerning perceptibility can only be answered on a case-by-case basis. There may well be perceptible distortion even in cases of smaller savings banks if their remaining on the market is contingent upon the contribution.

A distortion of competition cannot be denied with the argument that financial institutions under public law in other member countries also operate under similar liability or deposit guarantee systems. This so-called retortion argument is not recognized, since EU law works on the principle that there are different conditions in the different member countries and provides for special proceedings under Community law to remove them.[360]

II. Impairment of international trade

The constituent fact of impairment of trade has significance independent of distortion of competition.361 An impairment of trade occurs in the event of an artificial impediment to imports or an artificial easing of exports.[362] Subsidies can boost the "export" of services to other member countries or impede the entry of such services into the German market by financial institutions from other member countries. What is decisive is whether, under the influence of the subsidy, trade within the Community in goods, services and payment transactions is developing or could develop differently than would be the case without the subsidy.[363] Thus there can also be an

[360] *Cf.* European Court of Justice dated 12-10-1969, Kommission/Frankreich, Rs.6 and 11/69, Judgement 1969, 523; European Court of Justice dated 7-2-1974, Italien/Kommission, Rs. 173/73, Judgement 1974, 709; *cf. Wenig* in v.d. Groeben/Thiesing/Ehlermann, Art. 92, marginal note 21.

[361] *Wenig* in v.d.Groeben/Thiesing/Ehlermann, Art. 92 marginal note 23; *v. Wallenberg* in Grabitz/Hilf Art. 92 EC Treaty marginal note 29.

[362] *Wenig* in v.d.Groeben/Thiesing/Ehlermann, Art. 92, marginal note 24.

[363] *Cf.* European Court of Justice dated 12-12-1967, "Brasserie de Haecht I", Rs. 23/67, Judgement 1967, 543, 556 on Art. 85; *cf. Wenig* in v.d.Groeben/Thiesing/Ehlermann, Art. 92, marginal note 24.

impairment of trade even if no change in the flow of trade has occurred, but without the subsidy a change would have occurred. The fitness for an impairment of trade is already sufficient, so that it does not depend on there being an actual impairment.[364] The prevailing view is that a specific degree of trade impairment is not required.[365]

Since every subsidy bolsters the financial strength of a company and thus changes its competitive position, the assumption is that there is an impairment of trade if the subsidy causes a potential distortion of competition.[366] The elements upon which that assumption is based must be specifically spelled out by the Commission.[367]

In the communiqué concerning *Crédit Lyonnais*, the Commission pointed out that the liberalization of financial services and the integration of financial markets have brought about a situation where trade within the European Union has become increasingly sensitive to distortions of competition.[368] The Commission considered a trade-impeding effect of a subsidy to be a given, since *Crédit Lyonnais* provided loans and other financial resources to companies that competed on the international markets and offered financial services in competition with other European financial institutions.

For the majority of *Landesbanken* an impairment of trade would exist with respect to refinancing on international financial markets, to the extent that in individual cases such refinancing would qualify as a subsidy. Such impairment of trade is possible relating to financial services of foreign competitors rendered domestically. A perceptible impairment of trade regularly must also be assumed with respect to the export of services abroad, since *Landesbanken* now have access to branch offices and interests in financial institutions in other member countries and refinance themselves by means

---

[364] *Müller-Graff* ZHR 152 (1988), pp. 403, 433; *Lefèvre,* p. 128; *v. Wallenberg* in Grabitz/Hilf Art. 92 EC Treaty, marginal note 30.

[365] *Müller-Graff* ZHR 152 (1988), pp. 403, 434; *v. Wallenberg* in Grabitz/Hilf Art. 92 EC Treaty, marginal note 31, with reference to the Philip Morris decision dated 9-17-1980, Rs. 730/79, Judgement 1980, 2671, 2688; a different view *Wenig* in v.d. Groeben/Thiesing/Ehlermann, Art. 92, marginal note 25.

[366] Decision of the Commission, OJ. L 106/89, p. 34; European Court of Justice dated 9-17-1980, "Philip Morris", Rs. 730/79, Judgement 1980, 2671; *cf. Koenig,* EuZW 1995, pp. 595, 601.

[367] *Wenig* in v.d. Groeben/Thiesing/Ehlermann, Art. 92, marginal note 26.

[368] Communiqué concerning Crédit Lyonnais, *loc. cit.,* p. 11, no. 6.

of securities offerings in foreign currencies.[369] The general use of the international competitive capacity of the *Landesbanken*[370] also suggests the assumption of an impairment of trade.

For savings banks, to the extent one assumes a subsidy, the effects on international trade would be possible only to a limited extent at best. Such effects are conceivable in border areas, to the extent that a savings bank maintains accounts for persons who live outside of the country. The extension of loans to residents of other member countries, to the extent this is even permitted under savings bank laws[371], has an effect on international trade. Further, the savings bank laws in some German states permit savings banks to establish branch offices in neighboring EU countries.[372] An impairment of trade could exist to the extent that a business partner of a savings bank simultaneously maintains business relationships with foreign financial institutions. In this respect it is a matter to be considered on a case-by-case basis.

The factual characteristic of the impairment of trade between member countries may well be fulfilled with respect to savings banks, but, as these particular facts demonstrate, only in exceptional cases.

---

[369] *Cf.* on the subject of Yen and US-dollar bonds of Landesbank Rheinland-Pfalz *Adam,* Der langfristige Kredit 1996, pp. 38, 40.

[370] *Cf.* among others *Sauer,* DlfK 1993, pp. 165ff.; *Werner Schmidt,* ZfgK 1996, p. 200.

[371] Several states have since established statutory requirements for the extension of foreign credits; *cf. Schlierbach,* pp. 142f. The question of whether the granting of a credit to a foreign country is permitted even without a specific legal authorization is disputed and must be rejected, *cf. Schlierbach,* pp. 138ff. On the establishment of branch offices outside of a jurisdiction of the founding body, see also *Stern/Nierhaus,* Das Regionalprinzip im öffentlich-rechtlichen Sparkassenwesen.

[372] For example § 1,2 SparkG North Rhine-Westphalia, § 1,3 SparkG Saarland.

I. Summary

I. Institutional burden and guarantor liability as subsidies?

1. Assumptions of sureties or guarantees must fundamentally be considered to be subsidies even absent a case of liability and absent a flow of funds.

2. The assumption of liability associated with guarantor liability and institutional burden is not a subsidy measure comparable to a surety or guarantee, but is rather an individual liability by virtue of business organization. The liability as such, as a product of the state's freedom in the choice of legal form, is not subject to subsidy supervision.

3. Neither is a subsidy demonstrated pursuant to the private investor concept. Private companies also voluntarily assume comparable liability for other companies. This is possible through the founding or acquisition of private partnerships as well as through comfort letters or covenants to cover losses, all of which are common in the private banking industry. These forms of voluntary assumption of liability on the part of private companies are comparable to guarantor liability and institutional burden, because they entail the comprehensive liability for all obligations of a subsidiary, and the liability is secondary.

The principle associated with the operation of public banks of profit realization rather than profit maximization does not preclude the qualification as the common market behavior of a private investor. In the context of the "reasonable investor" standard that is recognized by both Commission and courts, the pursuit of commercial objectives other than short-term profit maximization has also been recognized. With respect to the subjective inclination to take risks and the assessment of future developments, one must accept broad entrepreneurial discretion on the part of the state, which also encompasses the operation of savings banks and *Landesbanken* together with all of the associated functions.

4. Finally, institutional burden and guarantor liability, as statutory obligations, correspond to some extent to the mandatory liability of a controlling shareholder pursuant to § 302 AktG and pursuant to the principles of material undercapitalization.

II. Institutional burden and guarantor liability as subsidies by virtue of refinancing advantages?

1. Guarantor liability and institutional burden, as liability by virtue of organization, are not subject to subsidy control. Thus for subsidy control as behavior control, the credit solvency of the guarantor is fundamentally irrelevant.

2. Savings banks are hardly active on international financial markets and are only rarely rated by the rating agencies. They do not enjoy any perceptible advantages, due to guarantor liability, in procuring non-bank deposits that would constitute a benefit in respect of improved financing on the basis of guarantor liability.

3. Whether guarantor liability constitutes an economic benefit of a *Landesbank* through an improvement of the refinancing terms is a question of an isolated case. There is no benefit for a large portion of the refinancing of *Landesbanken* by means of *covered* bonds. For naked bonds a benefit is hardly quantifiable. The stand-alone rating used for purposes of quantification is based on the hypothetical exclusion of liability mechanisms and thus is a purely subjective assessment. Contrary to the traditional rating, it does not enjoy increasing long-term acceptance on the part of investors and cannot be subject to any market control. Even the influence of traditional ratings on loan decisions is still quite small on the European capital markets where *Landesbanken* are primarily active. Both the criteria of the stand-alone rating itself as well as its comparability with the standards of the traditional rating are unclear. To the extent that a quantification is possible at all, it would have to take into consideration numerous factors.

A benefit for public companies over private companies due to the liability of the state cannot be assumed to the extent that a de facto state liability through support in a crisis situation is also possible for private banks. However, the de facto liability of the state in accordance with the principle of "too big to fail" has a lower degree of intensity than the statutory guarantor liability for public banks.

Accordingly, refinancing advantages can only be seen as a benefit in individual cases.

4. As a rule, no subsidy exists even pursuant to the private investor concept. A private investor would have provided a subsidiary a comparable assumption of liability for purposes of improving financing opportunities.

As a financing measure for a subsidiary, a private company can make it easier to acquire outside capital by providing guarantees instead of contributing its own capital or capital from outside sources. Among other ways, this can be accomplished by means of sureties or by assuming unlimited liability in the form of a comfort letter, a covenant to cover losses or as a liable partner.

The choice that is possible for private companies between the assumption of liability and a capital contribution with the option of support for their subsidiaries without any or with only slight encumbrances on their liquidity or balance sheet must also be open to the state within the framework of its broad entrepreneurial discretion. An assumed better credit solvency of the guarantor by virtue of its "unlimited resources" does not stand in the way of the private investor test. The behavior of a market-oriented investor has no connection with the credit solvency of the party assuming the liability.

5. The absence of a commission on guarantee could be used to establish the presence of a subsidy. As a rule, however, one must assume that for private companies, too, a direct consideration is normally dispensed with if liability is assumed for a subsidiary.

III. Actual contributions of capital as subsidies?

1. In principle, an actual contribution of capital to a savings bank or *Landesbank* constitutes an economic benefit.

2. A provision of capital in the execution of institutional burden is consistent with Article 92,1 EC Treaty, if a reasonable private investor would have done likewise.

This presupposes at a minimum the long-term profitability prospects of the bank. Capital transfers by a private investor are conceivable even without prospects of a justifiable return for purposes of image cultivation of the group or to make it possible to cease business operations under favorable terms.

One can derive from the statutory provisions governing institutional burden that these requirements of the private investor test as a rule are met. For they permit continued operation and thus a capital contribution only if the fulfillment of the legally mandated functions – of which sound management is one – is ensured. To this extent institutional burden is coupled with profitability prospects.

Outside these parameters of institutional burden, a contribution of capital, just as a continuation of liability, is to be seen as a subsidy and thus is prohibited to the extent that there are no special reasons for the permissibility of the subsidy.

IV. Special features of the banking sector: Compatibility of subsidization " to relieve a major economic disturbance" (Art. 92,3 (c) EC Treaty)

A general banking crisis would constitute a major economic disturbance within the meaning of Article 92,3 (c) EC Treaty. Given a financial institution of sufficient size, one can assume the approval of the subsidy because private banks would also receive state support in accordance with the principle of "too big to fail".

Bibliography

Adam, Klaus G., Refinanzierung im Wandel – das Beispiel der Landesbank Rheinland-Pfalz, Der langfristige Kredit, 1996, p. 38.

Beier/Heuser, Geldmarktfonds, Ärger mit der Sicherheit, Das Wertpapier 6/1995, p. 12.

Bieg, Hartmut, Bankbilanzen und Bankaufsichtsrecht, Munich 1983.

Blaurock, Uwe, Einfluß im Unternehmen und die gesellschaftsrechtliche Haftungsstruktur, Festschrift für Walter Stimpel, Berlin and others 1985, p. 553.

Breuer, Rolf-E. Zur Idee eines europäischen Rating, WM 1991, p. 1109.

Caspari, Manfred, Die Beihilferegeln des EWG- und EGKS-Vertrags und ihre Anwendung, Vortrag vor der Wirtschaftsvereinigung Eisen- und Stahlindustrie, Düsseldorf 1985.

Ciresa, Meinhard, Beihilfenkontrolle und Wettbewerbspolitik in der EG, Cologne and others 1992.

Claussen, Bernd, Teilprivatisierung kommunaler Sparkassen?, Ökonomische und rechtliche Rahmenbedingungen für eine Beteiligung Privater an kommunalen Kreditinstituten, Baden-Baden 1990.

Dennig, Ulrike, *Landesbanken* unter Privatisierungszwängen, Wirtschaftsdienst 1995, p. 210.

Deringer, Arved, Bericht für die Semaine de Bruges 1968, p. 387.

Dörries, Georg, Zur Rechtsstellung von *Landesbanken* unter besonderer Berücksichtigung der Westdeutschen Landesbank, Frankfurt a.M. 1988.

Ebenroth, Carsten Thomas/Daum, Thomas, Die rechtlichen Aspekte des Ratings von Emittenten und Emissionen, WM 1992, Supplement 5, p. 1.

Emmerich, Volker, Neues zur Zulässigkeit der wirtschaftlichen Betätigung der öffentlichen Hand, AG 1985, p. 293.

Engel, Wolfgang, Grenzen und Formen der mittelbaren Kommunalverwaltung, Cologne 1981.

Everling, Oliver,

- Credit Rating durch internationale Agenturen, 1981.
- Ratingagenturen weltweit, Die Bank 1991, p. 151.
- Projektgesellschaft für europäisches Rating, Die Bank 1991, p. 308.
- Bestimmungsgründe des langfristigen Rating, Die Bank 1991, p. 608.

Forsthoff, Ernst, Lehrbuch des Verwaltungsrechts, Vol. 1: Allgemeiner Teil, 10th edition, Munich 1973.

Gerke, Jürgen, Die wirtschaftliche Betätigung der Gemeinden, Jura 1985, p. 349.

Geßler/Hefermehl, Aktiengesetz, Kommentar von Ernst Geßler, Wolfgang Hefermehl, Ulrich Eckardt, Bruno Kropff, Vol. 2, Munich 1973, 1974.

Gleske, Christoph L., Wettbewerb öffentlicher und privater Kreditinstitute in Deutschland, Rechtsgrundlagen und Rechtsentwicklungen, Baden-Baden 1996.

Götz, Volkmar, Recht der Wirtschaftssubventionen, Munich 1966.

Grabitz, Eberhard/Hilf, Meinhard (eds.), Kommentar zum EWG-Vertrag, loose-leaf edition, status as of May 1995.

von der Groeben, Hans/Thiesing, Jochen/Ehlermann, Claus Dieter (eds.), Kommentar zum EWG-Vertrag, 4th edition, Baden-Baden 1991.

Gromoll, Bernhard, Rechtliche Grenzen der Privatisierung öffentlicher Aufgaben: untersucht am Beispiel kommunaler Dienstleistungen, Munich 1982.

Gruson, Michael/Schneider, Uwe H., The German *Landesbanken*, Columbia Business Law Review 1995, p. 337.

Gutsch, Hans-Martin, Die Rechtsstellung der Postbank im nationalen und europäischen Bankenwettbewerb, Eine verfassungs- und wettbewerbsrechtliche Analyse, Baden-Baden 1994.

Jung, Hans, Allgemeine Betriebswirtschaftslehre, Munich 1994.

Habersack, Mathias, Patronatserklärungen ad incertas personas, ZIP 1996, p. 257.

Hachenburg/Ulmer, Gesetz betreffend die Gesellschaft mit beschränkter Haftung, GmbHG, founded by Max Hachenburg, Peter Ulmer (ed.), 8th edition 1992.

Hedrich, Carl-Christoph, Die Privatisierung der Sparkassen: Ein Beitrag zu institutionellen Problemen der Deregulierung, Baden-Baden 1993, pp. 94ff.

Hellingman, K., State participation as state aid under Article 92 of the EEC Treaty: The Commission's guidelines, CMLR 1986, p. 111.

Hidien, Jürgen, Gemeindliche Betätigung rein erwerbswirtschaftlicher Art und „öffentlicher Zweck" kommunaler Wirtschaftsunternehmen, Berlin 1981.

Hoppe, Werner, Zur Diskussion um den Haftungszuschlag für die kommunalen Sparkassen, DVBl. 1982, p. 45.

Hüffer, Uwe, Aktiengesetz, 2nd edition, Munich 1995.

Kirchhof, Ferdinand, Schuldübergang und Haftung bei der Privatisierung der Postunternehmen, NvwZ 1994, p. 1041.

Klüpfel, Wolfgang/Gaberdiel, Heinz, Das Sparkassenrecht in Baden-Württemberg, Kommentar zum Sparkassengesetz, Part 1, 3rd edition, Stuttgart 1992.

Koenig, Christian,

- Begründen Anstaltslast und Gewährträgerhaftung unabhängig von ihrer Kodifizierung tragfähige Kreditmerkmale öffentlicher Finanzinstitute?, WM 1995, p. 821.

- öffentlich-rechtliche Anstaltslast und Gewährträgerhaftung als staatliche Beihilfen gem. Artikel 92 EC Treaty?, EuZW 1995, p. 595.

Kommission, Mitteilung der Kommission an die Mitgliedstaaten, Anwendung der Artikel 92 und 93 EWG-Vertrag und des Artikels 5 der Kommissionsrichtlinie 80/723/EWG über öffentliche Unternehmen in der verarbeitenden Industrie, Abl. C 307/3 dated 11-13-1993, cited as: Communiqué of the Commission on public companies.

Korndörfer, Wolfgang, Allgemeine Betriebswirtschaftslehre, 11th edition 1996.

Krümmel, Hans-Jakob, Bankpolitische Normen und ihre Wirkungen auf das Bankgeschäft, Kredit und Kapital 1975, p. 524.

Larenz, Karl / Canaris, Claus-Wilhelm, Schuldrecht II/2, 13th edition 1994.

Lefèvre, Dieter, Staatliche Ausfuhrförderung und das Verbot wettbewerbsverfälschender Beihilfen in EWG-Vertrag, 1977.

Lenz, Carl Otto, EG-Vertrag, Kommentar, 1995.

Lwowski, Hans-Jürgen/Groeschke, Peer, Die Konzernhaftung der 302, 303 AktG als atypische Sicherheit?, WM 1994, p. 613.

Mertens, Hans-Joachim, in: Kölner Kommentar zum Aktiengesetz, Vol. 2, 2nd edition 1989.

Mestmäcker, Ernst-Joachim, Staat und Unternehmen im europäischen Gemeinschaftsrecht – Zur Bedeutung von Art. 90 EWGV, RabelsZ 1988, p. 526.

Michalski, Lutz, Die Patronatserklärung, WM 1994, p. 1229.

Mösbauer, Heinz, Staatsaufsicht über die Wirtschaft, Cologne and others 1990.

Möschel, Wernhard,

- Das Wirtschaftsrecht der Banken, Die währungs-, bankaufsichts-, kartell- und EWG-rechtliche Sonderstellung der Kreditinstitute, 1972.

- Wurzeln der Bankenaufsicht, in: Festschrift für Theodor Heinsius, 1991, p. 575.
- Banken und Wettbewerb, in: Unternehmen, Recht und Wirtschaftsordnung: Festschrift für Peter Raisch zum 70. Geburtstag, Karsten Schmidt (ed.), 1995, p. 469.
- Privatisierung der Sparkassen, Zu den jüngsten Vorschlägen der Monopolkommission, WM 1993, p. 93.

Monopolkommission, Hauptgutachten XI, 1994/1995, BT-Drucks. 13/5309.

Müller, Nikolaus, Rechtsformenwahl bei der Erfüllung öffentlicher Aufgaben (Institutional choice), Cologne 1993.

Müller-Graff, Peter-Christian, Die Erscheinungsformen der Leistungssubventionstatbestände aus wirtschaftsrechtlicher Sicht, ZHR 151 (1988), p. 403.

Mura, Jürgen,

- Zur Geschichte des deutschen Sparkassenrechts von den Anfängen bis 1945, Sparkasse 1983, p. 69.
- Zur Geschichte des Spargeschäfts der Sparkassen von den Anfängen bis 1945, Sparkasse 1995, p. 88.

Nicolaysen, Gert, Subventionen für öffentliche Unternehmen und Wettbewerb im Gemeinsamen Markt, in: Börner, Bodo, Neundörfer, Konrad (eds.): Recht und Praxis der Beihilfen im Gemeinsamen Markt, 1984, p. 111.

Nicklisch, Fritz, Rechtsfragen der Einlagensicherung im Kreditgewerbe, Frankfurt 1979.

Nierhaus, Michael, Gutachtliche Stellungnahme zur Abgrenzung zwischen Trägerschaft und Eigentum an öffentlich-rechtlichen Sparkassen sowie zur Privatisierung der Sparkassen, Constance 1992.

Oebbecke, Janbernd, Rechtsfragen der Eigenkapitalausstattung der kommunalen Sparkassen, Siegburg 1980.

Petersen, Asger, Die Tatbestandsmerkmale „Beihilfe“ und „Wettbewerbsverfälschung“ in Artikel 92 EC Treaty aus der Sicht der Europäischen Kommission, in: EU-Beihilfenpolitik: Die Tatbestandsmerkmale des Artikels 92 Absatz 1 EG-Vertrag, Bundesverband der Deutschen Industrie e.V., Cologne 1994, p. 9.

Pohl, Hans, (ed.) Europäische Bankengeschichte, Frankfurt 1993.

Preißinger, Eberhard, Die Privilegierung öffentlicher Unternehmen, Dissertation Bayreuth 1990.

Püttner, Günter,
- Aktuelle Probleme des Verwaltungsprivatrechts im Organisationsbereich, JA 1980, p. 218.
- Besprechung der Monographie J. Oebbeckes, Rechtsfragen der Eigenkapitalausstattung der kommunalen Sparkassen, DVBl. 1981, p. 844.
- Zur Eigenkapitalausstattung der Sparkassen – insb. zur Verfassungsmässigkeit der Nichtanerkennung der Gewährträgerhaftung als Eigenkapitalsurrogat, Rechtsgutachten, 1983.
- Die öffentlichen Unternehmen, 2nd edition, Stuttgart 1985.

Raffée, H. / Fritz, W., Dimension und Konsistenz der Führungskonzeption von Industrieunternehmen – Ergebnisse einer empirischen Untersuchung, in; ZfbF 1992 No. 4, p. 303.

Raiser, Thomas, Recht der Kapitalgesellschaften, 2nd edition 1991.

von Randow, Philipp,
- Rating und Regulierung, ZBB 1995, p. 140.
- Rating und Wettbewerb, ZBB 1996, p. 85.

Rehm, Hannes, öffentlich-rechtliche Sparkassen: Privatisierung, weil erfolgreich im Wettbewerb?, WM 1993, p. 133.

Reischauer/Kleinhans, Kreditwesengesetz (KWG), Kommentar, founded by Friedrich Reischauer und Joachim Kleinhans, Berlin 1963 ff.

Rengeling, Hans Werner, Das Beihilferecht der Europäischen Gemeinschaften, in: Börner, Bodo, Neundörfer, Konrad (eds.): Recht und Praxis der Beihilfen im Gemeinsamen Markt, 1984, p. 23.

Rudo, Joachim, Book review of: Gutsch, Hans-Martin, Die Rechtsstellung der Postbank im nationalen und europäischen Bankenwettbewerb, Eine verfassungs- und wettbewerbsrechtliche Analyse, ZHR 159 (1995), p. 497

Rümker, Dietrich, Probleme der Anstaltslast und Gewährträgerhaftung bei öffentlich-rechtlichen Kreditinstituten, Festschrift für Ernst C. Stiefel, 1987, p. 607.

Sauer, Hans Dietmar, Die L-Bank als Geschäftsbank – eine Mischung von Markt und Aufgabe?, DlfK 1993, p. 165.

Scherer, Peter/Schödermeier, Martin, Staatliche Beihilfen und Kreditgewerbe, ZBB 1996, p. 165.

Schina, Despina, State Aids under the EEC Treaty, Articles 92 to 94, Oxford 1987.

Schlierbach, Helmut, Das Sparkassenrecht in der Bundesrepublik und in Berlin West, 3rd edition, Stuttgart 1994.

Schmidt, Dirk, Die Anstalt des öffentlichen Rechts als sozialstaatlich adäquate Unternehmensform für Sparkassen und öffentliche Banken, in: Banken und öffentlicher Auftrag, Bernd Lüthge (ed.), Bonn 1995.

Schmidt, Karsten,

- Gesellschaftsrecht, 2nd edition, Cologne and others 1991.
- Insolvenzrisiko und gesellschaftsrechtliche Haftung – Die Unternehmensinsolvenz als Bewährungsprobe des Gesellschaftsrechts, JZ 1985, p. 301.
- Die isolierte Verlustdeckungszusage unter verbundenen Unternehmen als Insolvenzabwendungsinstrument, in: Handelsrecht und Wirtschaftsrecht in der Bankpraxis, Festschrift für Winfried Werner, Berlin and others 1984, p. 777.

Schmidt, Reiner, öffentliches Wirtschaftsrecht, Allg. Teil, 1990.

Schmidt, Werner, Die SüdwestLB im Investment Banking, ZfgK 1996, p. 200.

Schmidt-Jortzig, Edzard,
- Kommunalrecht, Stuttgart 1982.
- Kommunale Organisationseinheit, Staatliche Organisationsgewalt und körperschaftliche Selbstverwaltung, Göttingen 1979.

Schneider, Uwe H.,
- Patronatserklärungen gegenüber der Allgemeinheit, ZIP 1989, p. 619.
- Kollektive konzernexterne und konzerninterne Patronatserklärungen, in Bankpolitik, finanzielle Unternehmensführung und die Theorie der Finanzmärkte, Festschrift für Hans-Jacob Krümmel, Berlin 1988, p. 351.
- Die Erweiterung des haftenden Eigenkapitals der öffentlich-rechtlichen Kreditinstitute durch Fusion, DB 1992, p. 769.

Schneider, Hannes/Busch, Torsten,
- Anstaltslast und Gewährträgerhaftung als Beihilfen im Sinne von Art. 92 EC Treaty?, EuZW 1995, p. 602.
- Swapgeschäfte der *Landesbanken* – Zugleich eine Entgegnung zu Christian Koenig, WM 1995, p. 317.

Scholz/Pitschas, Kriterien für die Wahl der Rechtsform, in Püttner (ed.), Handbuch der kommunalen Wissenschaft und Praxis, Vol. 5.

Schroeder, Dietrich, Rating für Bausparkassen?, Der langfristige Kredit 1995, p. 6.

Schwark, Eberhard, Einlagensicherung bei Banken, NJW 1974, p. 1849.

Seidel, Martin, EG-Binnenmarkt und öffentliche Unternehmen, in: Gröner/Schüller, Die Europäische Integration als ordnungspolitische Aufgabe, 1993, p. 343.

Serfling, Klaus/Pries, Andreas, Möglichkeiten und Grenzen des Rating, Die Bank 1990, p. 381.

Soukop, Karl, Die Mittelzuführungen an öffentliche Unternehmen im Rahmen der Beihilfeaufsicht der EU-Kommission, ZogU 1995, p. 16.

Standard & Poor's Ratings Handbook April 1995.

Stecher, Reiner „Harte" Patronatserklärungen – Rechtsdogmatische und praktische Probleme, Cologne 1978.

Stern, Klaus/Nierhaus, Michael, Die kommunalen Sparkassen, Verfassungs- und verwaltungsrechtliche Probleme, in: Schriften des Vereins für Kommunalwissenschaften e.V. Berlin, Vol. 34, Stuttgart and others 1972.

Stern, Klaus/Nierhaus, Michael, Das Regionalprinzip im öffentlich-rechtlichen Sparkassenwesen, Seine Geltung und Reichweite im Sparkassenorganisations- und Sparkassengeschäftsrecht, Heidelberg 1991.

Stimpel, Walter, Durchgriffshaftung bei der GmbH, in: Bilanz- und Konzernrecht, Festschrift für Reinhard Goerdeler, Düsseldorf 1987, p. 601.

Strombeck, Hans-Herbert, Die Banken der Bürgen, Die Bank 1995, p. 80.

Thode, Bernd,
- Der öffentliche Auftrag der *Landesbanken*, ZfgK 1994, p. 172.
- Zur Gewährträgerhaftung und Anstaltslast bei Sparkassen und *Landesbanken*, Sparkasse 1994, p. 134.

Tiedeken, Hans, Sparkassen und Kommunen, Sparkasse 1984, p. 286.

Twiehaus, Uwe, Die öffentlich-rechtlichen Kreditinstitute, Göttingen 1965.

Unknown author, „Konkurs unmöglich", Der Spiegel dated 4-8-1996, p. 102.

Wagner, Klaus, Die internationale Tätigkeit der Banken als aufsichtsrechtliches Problem, Baden-Baden 1982.

v. Wallenberg, Gabriela, Die Vereinbarkeit der staatlichen Finanzierung öffentlich-rechtlicher Fernsehanstalten mit Art. 92 EC Treaty, in: Gedächtnisschrift für Eberhard Grabitz, Albrecht Randelzhover (ed.), Munich 1995, p. 867.

Weides, Peter/Bosse, Burkhard Roderich, Rechtsprechung zum Sparkassenrecht, Part I, 1981.

Wettbewerbsenquête, Bericht der Bundesregierung über die Untersuchung der Wettbewerbsverschiebungen im Kreditgewerbe und über eine Einlagensicherung, Drucksache V/3500, 1968.

Wolf, Hans J./Bachof, Otto/Stober, Rolf, Verwaltungsrecht II, 5th edition, Munich 1987.

Wüst, Günther, Die unzureichende Eigenkapitalausstattung bei Beschränkthaftern, JZ 1995, p. 990.

MIX
Papier aus verantwortungsvollen Quellen
Paper from responsible sources
FSC® C105338

If you have any concerns about our products,
you can contact us on
ProductSafety@springernature.com

In case Publisher is established outside the EU,
the EU authorized representative is:
Springer Nature Customer Service Center GmbH
Europaplatz 3, 69115 Heidelberg, Germany

Printed by Libri Plureos GmbH
in Hamburg, Germany